Queen Victoria's Colonial Troops, 1837–1901

Gabriele Esposito is a military historian who works as a freelance author and researcher for some of the most important publishing houses in the military history sector. In particular, he is an expert specializing in uniformology: his interests and expertise range from the ancient civilizations to modern post-colonial conflicts. During recent years, he has conducted and published several researches on the military history of the Latin American countries, with special attention on the War of the Triple Alliance and the War of the Pacific. He is among the leading experts on the military history of the Italian Wars of Unification and the Spanish Carlist Wars. His books and essays are published on a regular basis by Osprey Publishing, Pen & Sword, Winged Hussar Publishing and Libreria Editrice Goriziana. He is also the author of numerous military history articles appearing in specialized magazines such as *Ancient Warfare Magazine, Medieval Warfare Magazine, The Armourer, History of War, Guerres et Histoire, Focus Storia* and *Focus Storia Wars*.

Queen Victoria's Colonial Troops, 1837–1901

Organization, Uniforms and Equipment

Gabriele Esposito

Pen & Sword
MILITARY

First published in Great Britain in 2025 by
Pen & Sword Military
An imprint of Pen & Sword Books Limited
Yorkshire – Philadelphia

Copyright © Pen & Sword Books Limited 2025

ISBN 978 1 03610 334 7

The right of Gabriele Esposito to be identified as
Author of this Work has been asserted by him in accordance
with the Copyright, Designs and Patents Act 1988.

A CIP catalogue record for this book is
available from the British Library.

All rights reserved. No part of this book may be reproduced, transmitted, downloaded, decompiled or reverse engineered in any form or by any means, electronic or mechanical including photocopying, recording or by any information storage and retrieval system, without permission from the Publisher in writing. NO AI TRAINING: Without in any way limiting the Author's and Publisher's exclusive rights under copyright, any use of this publication to "train" generative artificial intelligence (AI) technologies to generate text is expressly prohibited. The Author and Publisher reserve all rights to license uses of this work for generative AI training and development of machine learning language models.

Typeset by Mac Style

The Publisher's authorised representative in the EU for product
safety is Authorised Rep Compliance Ltd., Ground Floor,
71 Lower Baggot Street, Dublin D02 P593, Ireland.
www.arccompliance.com

For a complete list of Pen & Sword titles please contact

PEN & SWORD BOOKS LIMITED
47 Church Street, Barnsley, South Yorkshire, S70 2AS, England
E-mail: enquiries@pen-and-sword.co.uk
Website: www.pen-and-sword.co.uk
or
PEN AND SWORD BOOKS
1950 Lawrence Road, Havertown, PA 19083, USA
E-mail: uspen-and-sword@casematepublishers.com
Website: www.penandswordbooks.com

Contents

Introduction		vi
Chapter 1	Canada	1
Chapter 2	West Indies	50
Chapter 3	Australia	61
Chapter 4	New Zealand	80
Chapter 5	South Africa	86
Chapter 6	India	105
Chapter 7	Asia	176
Chapter 8	Africa	196
Chapter 9	The Mediterranean	222
Bibliography		228
Index		230

Introduction

The main aim of this book is to present a detailed overview of the history, organization and uniforms of British colonial troops during the period 1815–1914. This period saw the ascendancy of Great Britain as the world's leading colonial power, following the end of the Napoleonic Wars. The military forces of all the British colonies will be taken into account, from the larger overseas possessions to the smaller ones. The first chapter will be devoted to Canada, Great Britain's large colony in North America; the second chapter will focus on the smaller British possessions in Central America (notably the islands collectively known as the West Indies) and in South America. Successive chapters will cover the various colonies that made up Australia; New Zealand; South Africa and the other nearby British colonial possessions that became part of it; the richest of all the British colonies, India; Britain's other Asian possessions (Ceylon, Burma, Singapore, Malay, Borneo, Hong Kong and Aden); the various British colonies in Western Africa, Central Africa and Eastern Africa; and the British overseas possessions located in the Mediterranean (Malta, Gibraltar, Ionian Islands and Cyprus). The uniforms of the various colonial contingents will be reproduced in the many colour pictures illustrating the written text and will be detailed in the relative captions.

Chapter 1

Canada

When the USA became independent in 1783, Britain was able to retain possession of Canada. This remained the largest colony of the British Crown at a time during which India was still administered by the private East India Company and Australia was only in the early phases of its colonization. From an administrative point of view, British Canada was divided as follows: Lower Canada, Upper Canada, Nova Scotia, New Brunswick, Newfoundland, Prince Edward Island and Cape Breton Island. The economies of all these territories had a particular role in the global commercial system created by Britain and were mostly based on the fur trade and fishing. Exploitation of forests for wood was also a very important activity: during the long wars against Revolutionary and Napoleonic France, Canada became vital for Britain as a source of high quality wood for building warships. In general, the territory of Canada was not as economically developed as that of the USA, but its population (albeit quite small) was made up of sturdy and courageous people. The troops garrisoning Canada until 1815 were of three different kinds: British regular units, Canadian Militia units and Canadian volunteer units. The militia system of Canada derived from the French colonial period and remained extremely efficient under the British, as the US Army learned to its cost during its attempted invasion of Canada in 1812. At the outbreak of the war with the USA, there were very few British regular units stationed in North America, consisting of just 6,034 men and including the following corps:

- 8th Regiment of Foot (1st Battalion in Canada, 2nd Battalion in Nova Scotia and New Brunswick)
- 41st Regiment of Foot
- 49th Regiment of Foot
- 100th Regiment of Foot
- Six companies of the 98th Regiment of Foot (in Nova Scotia)
- Four companies of the 99th Regiment of Foot (in Nova Scotia)
- 10th Royal Veteran Battalion
- Detachments of the Royal Artillery
- Detachments of the Royal Engineers

2   Queen Victoria's Colonial Troops, 1837–1901

- Detachments of the Royal Military Artificers/Royal Sappers and Miners
- Canadian Fencible Infantry
- Nova Scotia Fencible Infantry
- New Brunswick Fencible Infantry
- Newfoundland Fencible Infantry

The core of the British troops in North America was represented by the 41st and 49th Regiments of Foot, which had been garrisoned in Canada for a long time. These two units had learned how to fight in the woods of North America and had a special relationship with the local population. Since 1688, the English Army had comprised a Corps of Invalids, made up of veteran soldiers who were no longer fit for active service but could still be employed for static or garrison duties. By the end of the eighteenth century, similar units existed in all the European armies and were sometimes called to serve during times of conflict. To become a member of the Corps of Invalids, a British veteran had to be chosen by the commissioners of the Royal Hospital in Chelsea, who analyzed the physical condition of all the veterans who were no longer fit for active service and decided if they could be employed as garrison troops or could only receive a pension from the state. The Corps of Invalids was organized into a varying number of independent infantry companies, which were scattered across Britain to garrison key points of the country. Thanks to the presence of the Invalids, a number of active military units could be freed from garrison duties and thus be available for overseas service. Before

Private of the St John's Volunteer Rangers from Newfoundland in 1815. The uniform is very similar to that of the contemporary riflemen of the British Army. (*ASKB Military Collection*)

Officers (left), NCO (centre) and privates (right) of the King's Royal Rifle Corps in 1825. Both the parade dress and service dress of officers are in the hussar style that was typical of the British rifle corps during the early nineteenth century. (*ASKB Military Collection*)

the outbreak of the war with Revolutionary France, the Corps of Invalids comprised around 7,000 veterans, who usually served as garrison troops for a period of service of six years. In 1802, following the Peace of Amiens with France, it was decided to reorganize the Corps of Invalids and give to its units the new denomination of Royal Garrison Battalions. In 1804, the new and definitive name of Royal Veteran Battalions was introduced, but the functions and structure of the reorganized units were not changed. Under the reforms of 1802, the various independent companies of invalids were grouped together to form battalions, which performed auxiliary duties like working in depots or performing administrative functions. In addition, in case of foreign invasion, they could protect British territory as static defence units. During the Napoleonic Wars, some battalions of veterans were also sent overseas and fought as auxiliary troops, such as the 10th Royal Veteran Battalion. The latter unit was created in December 1806 on the Isle of Wight, with volunteers coming from the other veteran battalions. From the outset, it was established for service in Canada rather than Britain. Members of the unit were promised a grant of land in North America upon their retirement. When the War of 1812 broke out between Great Britain and the United States, the 10th Royal Veteran Battalion was one of the first units that fought for the defence of Canada. In April 1813, a small group of its members – just seventeen in number – were organized to form a Mounted Veterans Corps, charged with maintaining communications between the various defensive posts in the Montreal area. The 10th Royal Veteran Battalion was disbanded in 1816. Overseas veteran corps included two companies active in the Caribbean and known as European Garrison Companies, plus two similar companies made up of

Private (left) and officers (right) of the King's Royal Rifle Corps in 1846. The two officers are wearing the service dress with peaked caps. (*ASKB Military Collection*)

black veterans known as Black Garrison Companies. One veteran company was also present at the Cape of Good Hope in South Africa, with another in New South Wales, Australia.

The Fencible Regiments were another category of foot troops that were included in the British Army. The term 'Fencibles' derived from the word 'defencible', these being static units formed specifically for the defence of a particular territory. They were fixed garrison corps, similar to the units of the territorial militia: since they were recruited on a local basis, they had strong links with their home territory, albeit being

Officer from the Queen's Light Dragoons of Montreal in 1846. This uniform, which is almost identical to that of the contemporary light dragoons of the British Army, was worn also by the Provincial Cavalry that existed until 1850. (*ASKB Military Collection*)

part of the British regular forces. Generally speaking, the Fencible Regiments were temporary units that were raised for active service only when Britain or some colonial territory was under threat of foreign invasion. They were made up of volunteers but were commanded by officers from the regular army. The Canadian Fencible Infantry was originally raised in Scotland from highlanders who wished to emigrate to Canada. In 1803, however, some misunderstandings regarding the terms of enlistment led to a mutiny of the recruits before their departure from Scotland. As a result of this, in 1804 only the commissioned officers of the unit and some NCOs were finally sent to North America, with orders to recruit the required rankers from the local colonists. Many of the Canadians who joined the unit were sons of Loyalists who had abandoned the Thirteen Colonies after they became independent from Britain and who had settled in southern Canada. The Nova Scotia Fencible Infantry, as its name suggests, was raised in Nova Scotia (a peninsula in eastern Canada) but was garrisoned in Newfoundland between 1805 and 1812. The original New Brunswick Fencible Infantry was transformed into the 104th Foot Regiment during 1810, after it volunteered for overseas service in 1808. To replace the original Fencible unit, another one having the same denomination and internal organization was raised in 1813 (which was disbanded like the other Canadian Fencibles in 1816). The Newfoundland Fencible Infantry was mostly recruited from expert fishermen and boatmen living on Newfoundland Island. Consequently, in 1812, five of its companies were sent to serve as marines on the Great Lakes. During the period 1815–1871, the following regular corps of the British Army were stationed in Canada:

- 1st Foot Guards (2nd Battalion 1838–1842, 1st Battalion 1862–1863)
- 2nd Foot Guards (2nd Battalion 1838–1842 and 1869)
- 3rd Foot Guards (2nd Battalion 1862–1864)
- 1st Regiment of Foot (2nd Battalion 1838–1839)
- 6th Regiment of Foot (2nd Battalion 1846–1847)
- 7th Regiment of Foot (1st Battalion 1807–1867, 2nd Battalion 1858–1868)
- 8th Regiment of Foot (1830–1833 and 1839–1841)
- 9th Regiment of Foot (1854–1857)
- 11th Regiment of Foot (1839–1840)
- 12th Regiment of Foot (1858–1861)
- 14th Regiment of Foot (1841–1848)
- 15th Regiment of Foot (1827–1840, 1st Battalion 1861–1870)
- 16th Regiment of Foot (1853–1857 and 1861–1870)
- 17th Regiment of Foot (1st Battalion 1855–1865, 2nd Battalion 1858–1868)
- 19th Regiment of Foot (1848–1851)
- 20th Regiment of Foot (detachments 1842–1853)
- 23rd Regiment of Foot (2nd Battalion 1858–1867)
- 24th Regiment of Foot (1829–1842)
- 26th Regiment of Foot (1853–1859)
- 29th Regiment of Foot (1867–1870)
- 30th Regiment of Foot (1841–1843 and 1861–1869)

- 32nd Regiment of Foot (1830–1841)
- 33rd Regiment of Foot (1840–1848)
- 34th Regiment of Foot (1830–1840)
- 36th Regiment of Foot (1830–1839)
- 37th Regiment of Foot (1814–1826 and 1839–1842)
- 38th Regiment of Foot (1848–1851)
- 39th Regiment of Foot (1856–1859)
- 43rd Regiment of Foot (1835–1846)
- 47th Regiment of Foot (1863–1868)
- 52nd Regiment of Foot (1823–1831)
- 53rd Regiment of Foot (1866–1870)
- 54th Regiment of Foot (detachments 1845–1854)
- 56th Regiment of Foot (1840–1842)
- 60th Regiment of Foot (1845–1847 and 1866–1871)
- 62nd Regiment of Foot (1857–1864)
- 63rd Regiment of Foot (1855–1865)
- 64th Regiment of Foot (1840–1842)
- 65th Regiment of Foot (detachments 1838–1841)
- 66th Regiment of Foot (1827–1841 and 1853–1856)
- 68th Regiment of Foot (1818–1829 and 1841–1844)
- 69th Regiment of Foot (1839–1842 and 1867–1870)
- 70th Regiment of Foot (1813–1827 and 1841–1843)
- 71st Regiment of Foot (1824–1832, 2nd Battalion 1842–1854)
- 72nd Regiment of Foot (1851–1854)
- 73rd Regiment of Foot (1838–1841)
- 74th Regiment of Foot (1818–1828 and 1841–1845)
- 76th Regiment of Foot (1814–1827 and 1853–1857)
- 77th Regiment of Foot (1846–1848)
- 78th Regiment of Foot (1867–1871)
- 79th Regiment of Foot (1825–1832 and 1848–1851)
- 81st Regiment of Foot (1822–1829)
- 82nd Regiment of Foot (1843–1847)
- 83rd Regiment of Foot (1838–1839)
- 84th Regiment of Foot (1870)
- 85th Regiment of Foot (1835–1842)
- 93rd Regiment of Foot (1838–1848)
- 96th Regiment of Foot (1825–1831)
- 98th Regiment of Foot (1814–1818)

- Rifle Brigade (1st Battalion 1826–1836, 2nd Battalion 1842–1852, 4th Battalion 1862–1871)
- 1st Dragoon Guards (1838–1844)
- 6th Dragoons (1861–1863)
- 21st Dragoons (1846–1850)
- 19th Light Dragoons (1811–1816)
- 7th Hussars (1838–1842)
- 13th Hussars (1866–1869)

In addition to the above, the British Army always deployed a number of Royal Artillery and Royal Engineers companies in the North American colonies. As is made clear by the list above, most of the British regiments of foot had a period of service in Canada during the period 1815–1871, highlighting that garrisoning North America effectively required significant resources of the British Army. Two British infantry units, in particular, had a history that was strongly related to North America: the 60th Regiment of Foot and the Rifle Brigade. The 60th Regiment was raised in 1756, mostly as a result of the disastrous defeat suffered by the British line infantry at the Battle of Monongahela during the French-Indian War in 1754. This clash took place in North America and saw the ambush of 1,300 British soldiers by a smaller force of French supported by Canadian Militiamen and natives, who

Uniforms of the Québec volunteer corps in 1837–1838, from left to right: private from the 1st Company of the Québec Light Infantry, private from the 4th Company of the Québec Light Infantry, private from the 2nd Company of the Québec Light Infantry and private of the Queen's Own Light Infantry of Québec. The greatcoats and the moccasins of these figures are those worn by the Francophone fur hunters of Canada. (*ASKB Military Collection*)

Uniforms of the Québec volunteer corps in 1837–1838, from left to right: private of the Royal Québec Volunteers and private of the Québec Highland Company. Note the use of the typical blue Highland bonnet. (*ASKB Military Collection*)

annihilated their opponents. The battle was a disaster for the British, who lost over 450 men during the ambush and proved wholly unable to deal with their enemy's skirmishing tactics in any way. The new light infantry unit created after the Battle of Monongahela was initially known as the 62nd Regiment of Foot 'Royal American', only adopting its definitive progressive number (the 60th) at a later date. Approval for the raising of such a regiment, as well as the necessary funds were, granted by the British Parliament in late 1755. The new unit comprised four battalions, each with 1,000 soldiers, and its main function was to counter the raids launched by the French and their native allies against the British settlements of the Thirteen Colonies. The regiment was recruited from colonists who already had experience of light infantry tactics as well as from foreigners who had hunting skills. In particular, the British Army was interested in recruiting experienced German or Swiss hunters and gamekeepers. In 1756, to allow such veteran personnel to be obtained, Parliament passed the Commissions to Foreign Protestants Act that permitted the recruiting of foreign officers from the German states and Swiss cantons. These could be employed in the new 62nd Foot, but could not rise above the rank of lieutenant colonel. In total, some fifty officers of the new regiment came from Germany or Switzerland.

The original idea behind the formation of the new unit had been by Jacques Prevost, a Swiss soldier and adventurer who was a personal friend of the Duke of Cumberland (second son of King George II). Prevost was an expert in forest warfare and one of the first to understand the combat potential of light infantry. The foreign officers of the regiment included two notable personalities: Henri Bouquet (who commanded the 1st Battalion) and Frederick Haldimand (who was in charge of the 2nd Battalion). Both these Swiss professionals made a great contribution to the development of light infantry doctrines within the British Army. Their forward-looking ideas included the introduction of rifled muskets among the rankers. During the French-Indian War, the 60th Foot fought with enormous courage during several of the most important engagements, earning a solid reputation and its famous motto '*Celer et Audax*' ('Swift and Bold'). In 1762, in order to keep its soldiers in the ranks of the British armed forces, Parliament passed the American Protestant Soldier Naturalization Act, which offered naturalization to all those foreign officers and soldiers who had already served under the Union Jack for at least two years. The 5th Battalion of the regiment was raised in 1797, using the soldiers of a German mercenary regiment (Hompesch's Mounted Riflemen) that had recently been disbanded. A 6th Battalion was added in 1799, formed from German recruits. Finally, another two battalions were raised during 1813 for service in the Americas during the War of 1812 against the USA. These last two battalions were recruited from German and Swiss prisoners of war who had been part of Napoleon's armies.

The 60th Regiment of Foot continued to be strongly linked to the Americas after the Napoleonic Wars, remaining the British foot regiment with the highest percentage of German or Swiss rankers for some decades. With the general demobilization of the British Army that followed the Battle of Waterloo, it was restructured on just two battalions, members of which were all equipped with rifled carbines. With the new denomination of the King's Royal Rifle Corps, assumed in 1830, the unit performed garrison duties for most of the mid-nineteenth century. When the Crimean War broke out, the British authorities decided to send the Rifle Brigade to the theatre of operations so the 60th Regiment did not participate in the hostilities. In 1855, however, it became apparent that the war with Russia was going to be fought on a larger scale, and the King's Royal Rifle Corps was expanded with the addition of two new battalions.

The Rifle Brigade could trace its origins back to January 1800, when several line infantry regiments of the British Army were ordered to send one captain, one lieutenant, one ensign, two sergeants, one corporal and thirty of their best privates to be trained as riflemen. The chosen men, who were the best marksmen of their respective units, made up a new independent corps of riflemen. The initial idea by the Duke of York – at that time overall commander of the British Army – was to train these elite soldiers as riflemen and send them back to their original units to act as the core for the formation of rifle companies in each line regiment. The temporary training unit that had just been created was named the Experimental Corps of Riflemen and was commanded by Colonel Coote Manningham, one of the British Army's leading experts in light infantry tactics. The new corps trained the riflemen by following Colonel Manningham's innovative ideas, which were published in 1800 as the 'Regulations for the Rifle Corps formed at Blachington Barracks under the command of Colonel Manningham'. Members of the Experimental Corps of Riflemen were trained to observe rigid and unthinking obedience to the orders received, in order to be more autonomous on the battlefield and create a special relationship based on mutual trust with their officers and NCOs. A new sense of comradeship was developed, with one 'soldier of merit' selected in each half-platoon to assume command of his squad when NCOs were absent and be in a privileged position to be promoted as corporal. The Experimental Corps of Riflemen comprised a total of just five companies, each of which was divided into two equally sized platoons, in turn divided into four squads. The members of each squad trained and lived together every day in order to develop a special personal relationship that would be of great use on the battlefield. Meritocracy was encouraged with every possible method, including prizes offered by officers to the best marksmen under their command. Training of the new experimental corps was intensive and comprised field exercises that were made as realistic as possible. The basic idea was to forge soldiers who would be able to think in a highly autonomous way and act very rapidly according to circumstances. Individual capabilities were fundamental in this regard, and thus only the best soldiers of the whole British infantry were admitted into the ranks of the Experimental Corps of Riflemen. Training included moving swiftly on broken terrain, surviving with the few food resources that an enemy countryside could offer, skirmishing on the open field, penetrating the enemy's lines without being noticed, launching surprise attacks to occupy enemy outposts, scouting for larger units during an advance and acting as a rearguard to cover a retreat. New recruits were gradually added to the Rifle Corps (this name having been introduced in October 1800), thanks to which the unit was expanded to become a battalion.

In February 1801, the Rifle Corps was transferred to the official establishment of the infantry and thus became a permanent unit, being officially transformed into a regiment and receiving the denomination of the 95th 'Rifle' Regiment in

Uniforms of the Québec volunteer corps in 1837–1838, from left to right: officer of the Québec Volunteer Cavalry and gunner of the Québec Volunteer Artillery. (*ASKB Military Collection*)

Uniforms of the Québec volunteer corps in 1837–1838, from left to right: NCO of the Québec Volunteer Artificers, private of the Québec Volunteer Engineers and private of the Québec Volunteer Sailors. (*ASKB Military Collection*)

1802. During the following years, the riflemen took part in all the most important campaigns fought by the British Army, always distinguishing themselves and winning an impressive number of awards. Due to their superior training and morale, they were usually employed as 'special forces' and often accomplished missions that seemed impossible on paper. By 1815, the establishment of the regiment consisted of three battalions. At the end of the Napoleonic Wars, the 95th Regiment retained its special status and peculiar methods of training, and in 1816 the three existing battalions were reorganized as the autonomous Rifle Brigade. This was later expanded to four battalions, each of which – like those of the King's Royal Rifle Corps – comprised eight companies. The four battalions were assembled into two regiments and in 1852 overall command of the Rifle Brigade was given to Prince Albert (consort of Queen Victoria), who did his best to preserve the excellent reputation of the unit. By the outbreak of the Crimean War, the Rifle Brigade was known as The Prince Consort's Own Rifle Brigade and had been reorganized as a single regiment with two battalions, each having twelve companies. Both battalions were sent to the Crimea, where they distinguished themselves in several of the bloodiest engagements, including the Alma, Inkerman and Sevastopol. At the outbreak of hostilities with Russia, another two battalions were created, making a total of four. Like the King's Royal Rifle Corps, the Rifle Brigade had a special connection with Canada because its members were trained and equipped to operate as elite light infantry in the woodlands of

14 Queen Victoria's Colonial Troops, 1837–1901

North America. During the period 1862–1871, the 4th Battalion of the Rifle Brigade acted as the guard of the Governor General of Canada and the Canadian government, being assigned to the garrison at Ottawa. In 1840, Lower Canada and Upper Canada were unified as a single colony; several years later, in 1867, they were joined by Nova Scotia (which included Cape Breton Island from 1820) and New Brunswick to form the new Dominion of Canada. Newfoundland and Prince Edward Island only later became part of the new Canadian state, remaining small autonomous British colonies for some time. With the birth of the Dominion of Canada, the British government – which had been sponsoring self-government in its North American territories for some time – progressively reduced its military presence in Canada in order to favour the development of a local system of self-defence. By 1871, all the British regular units garrisoning Canada had left the country, except for a few that remained in Halifax to garrison the Royal Navy base there. As a result, the Canadian colonial forces had to be completely reorganized in order to replace the British regulars; the 4th Battalion of the Rifle Brigade played

Fur hunter of the Hudson's Bay Company in 1835. The militiamen of the Red River Volunteers and the Victoria Voltigeurs were dressed in Francophone style like this figure. (*Colour plate by Patricio Greve Moller, copyright of Gabriele Esposito*)

Uniforms of the militia of New Brunswick in 1845, from left to right: line infantry officer in summer undress uniform, line infantry officer in winter parade uniform, light infantry officer in winter parade uniform (from the militia of Saint John) and officer of the Queen's New Brunswick Rangers. (*ASKB Military Collection*)

an important role during this phase, retraining the Canadian Militia units from 1867 onwards.

In Canada, like in the USA, the militia was formed from all the able-bodied men who were eligible for military service according to their age. Since the foundation of the first French settlements in the early decades of the seventeenth century, the Canadians had to adopt a form of local military organization in order to repulse violent raids by various native tribes. This system continued during the eighteenth century, with the Canadian Militiamen fighting with great valour against the British and their native allies during the French-Indian War. Unlike what happened in the Thirteen Colonies, the militia units of French Canada were under strict control from the central authorities of the colony. Generally speaking, the Canadian Militias had fewer men than their American equivalents, but each individual had superior military capabilities. Most of the settlers in Canada were huntsmen and thus were used to travelling long distances in the worst of weather conditions. They had extensive knowledge of the vast forests and plains surrounding them and were all excellent marksmen, employing rifled muskets exactly like the American colonists. Thanks to their mobility and capacity to organize ambushes, the Canadian Militiamen were able to fight against the natives on almost equal terms: they were experts in guerrilla warfare and often launched surprise attacks. The Canadian Militiamen were also able to operate during winter and had all equipment necessary to survive extremely cold temperatures. Rivers and lakes were no barriers to them, as they were also skilful in the use of canoes. The British inherited the militia system from the French after conquering Canada in 1763 and did nothing to change it. Instead, they tried to 'regularize' as much as possible the Canadian Militia units in order to transform them into a proper auxiliary army that could support their regular forces. By around 1800, most of Canada's population consisted of Francophone settlers, who had always been extremely loyal to France until the very last days of the French-Indian War. Consequently, at the outbreak of the War of 1812 with the USA, the British authorities feared that these men may refuse to serve in the militia or revolt against the Crown. However, the Canadian colonists all remained loyal to Britain, with no distinction between the Francophones and Anglophones. The Canadians already considered their territory a 'nation', and the foreign aggression of the USA did nothing but augment their patriotic feelings. In 1815, from an administrative point of view, the territory of Canada was divided in two major provinces: Lower Canada and Upper Canada. In addition to these, there were also Indian Department and the smaller Atlantic Colonies. The Indian Department comprised all the unsettled lands located west of the Great Lakes, while the Atlantic Colonies were formed from the smaller British colonies that were situated on the Atlantic coast (Nova Scotia, New Brunswick, Newfoundland, Prince Edward Island and Cape Breton Island).

The province of Lower Canada corresponded to the former territory of New France and comprised most of the Francophone settlers in British North America. It had a much larger population than Upper Canada and comprised the three most important cities of British North America: Québec, Montreal and Trois-Rivières. The militia of this colony included an active force (known as the Select Militia) and a reserve one (the Sedentary Militia). The Select Militia was activated only in case of foreign menace and consisted of the best elements from the Sedentary Militia. When a unit was called to serve, no matter if coming from the Select Militia or Sedentary Militia, it received the further title of 'Embodied' (meaning it was attached to the regulars). In 1812, as part of the mobilization for the war against the USA, a total of 6,500 militiamen were activated to form the Select Embodied Militia of Lower Canada. This was initially structured on four infantry battalions, each with 800 men, which were to serve for a period of two years. After war was declared, a 5th Battalion was

NCOs of the Royal Canadian Rifle Regiment; the figure on the left is from 1854 and the figure on the right from 1869. The dress of the regiment was modelled on that of the King's Royal Rifle Corps. (*ASKB Military Collection*)

added on 21 September. In late June 1813, the flank companies of the five existing units were grouped together to form two independent battalions of light infantry, known as the Militia Light Infantry Battalions. These were temporary units and thus were dissolved on 25 November 1813, with the various companies returning to their original battalions. A 6th Battalion was formed on 28 February 1813 and briefly served as the garrison of Québec, having a smaller establishment compared with the existing units and being disbanded in September 1814. In March 1814, the 5th Battalion was reorganized as an independent light infantry unit and received the denomination of the Canadian Chasseurs. The original four units continued to serve with distinction until the end of the war, being discharged only on 1 March 1815. As it was directly threatened by the US invasion, Lower Canada also mobilized its Sedentary Militia during the hostilities of 1812–1815. This numbered some 54,000 militiamen, who were organized in two different ways according to their ethnic origins. The Sedentary Militia of the Francophone communities had the parish company as their basic unit with each parish (generally corresponding to a village) providing an infantry company commanded by a captain. The various parish companies were assembled into three divisions, which

Private of the Enrolled Pensioners in 1852. This dark blue uniform with peaked cap was worn by all the invalid corps of the British Army. (*ASKB Military Collection*)

had more or less the same numerical establishment as a regiment. Each of the three districts that made up the province of Lower Canada (Québec, Montreal and Trois-Rivières) had one of these divisions. The few Anglophone settlers of Lower Canada had a different military organization. They lived in the Eastern Townships, which had been settled by Loyalist colonists during the American Revolution, thus forming an independent district. The Eastern Townships District had a militia that was organized according to counties, copying the traditional British system. Each county, according to its population, was to provide one or more infantry regiments, each with six battalions. A battalion could sometimes have an attached troop of cavalry. While the system described above was generally followed by the Sedentary Militia in rural areas, in the major cities of Québec, Montreal and Trois-Rivières the situation was completely different. These important centres had several infantry battalions of urban militiamen. Québec had three infantry battalions: the 1st and 2nd were made up of Francophone citizens, while the 3rd comprised Anglophone militiamen. Montreal also had three infantry battalions: the 1st contained Anglophone citizens, while the 2nd and 3rd comprised Francophone militiamen. The urban militia of Trois-Rivières consisted of a single infantry battalion. Québec's battalions (created in 1803) had flank companies like those of the regular military, these comprising chosen volunteers rather than ordinary militiamen. The battalions from Montreal had flank companies too, which were assembled for some time in order to form a temporary elite battalion. The urban militias of Québec and Montreal each also included one troop of cavalry and two companies of artillery, which were all formed from well-educated gentlemen and volunteers. The urban militias took part in no significant military actions during the War of 1812 and were disbanded as soon as the American menace vanished in 1815.

The province of Upper Canada had initially mostly been inhabited by Loyalist Americans who abandoned the Thirteen Colonies during the Revolution against British rule. It saw much of the combat operations of the 1812–1815 war taking place on its territory and thus suffered greatly from the devastation caused by the opposing armies. Despite having a smaller population than Lower Canada, Upper Canada made a significant contribution to the British war effort. Geographically, Upper Canada comprised a vast territory located between the western border of Québec province and the city of Windsor on Lake Huron. In total, the province contained eight districts, which were divided into several counties. The Sedentary Militia of Upper Canada was much younger than that of Lower Canada, having been organized for the first time in 1793. Similarly to what happened in the Eastern Townships District of Lower Canada, it was based on county regiments of infantry that consisted of a single battalion with ten companies. In March 1812, some months before the outbreak of the war with the USA, each battalion was enlarged with the addition of two flank companies made up of volunteers under 40 years of age. On 18 March 1813, a single battalion of Select Embodied Militia with ten companies was formed in Upper Canada, its 500 men comprising the best elements of the Sedentary Militia. The companies of this battalion took part in several important engagements of the war and proved to be units of high quality, comparable to those of British regular units. In 1812, the Indian Department of Canada was mostly unsettled, being defended by just a few forts, so very few military units were raised from it. The only inhabitants of the Indian Department were '*voyageurs*' (hunters) and fur traders, who were partly regularized in order to serve in military corps. The first unit to be formed in the Indian Department was the Michigan Fencibles, a small infantry company of just forty-five men that was created by recruiting *voyageurs* and fur traders. Like the other Fencible units, it was formed to garrison a specific area of territory, being

Uniforms of the Montreal Rifle Rangers in 1854, from left to right: NCO, officers and privates. The soft peaked cap was comfortable to wear on campaign. (*ASKB Military Collection*)

Officer (left) and NCO (right) of the Canadian Militia's rifle companies in 1862. (*ASKB Military Collection*)

stationed in the strategic position of Fort Mackinac. The unit was disbanded at the end of the conflict, on 28 June 1815. In July 1814, other Francophone *voyageurs* were recruited in the Indian Department in order to form volunteer companies: these became known as Mississippi Volunteers and initially consisted of just one company with sixty-five men. Apparently, this volunteer corps also included a small detachment of artillery. The Indian Department ceased to exist in 1860, when its territories were put under direct Canadian administration.

In 1812, the general militia of Nova Scotia consisted of twenty-six infantry battalions, known by the name of the county in which they were formed. At that time Nova Scotia had twelve counties, and each of them formed a number of infantry battalions according to its population. Some of the infantry battalions had attached artillery companies; in addition, from 1813, each of them had two additional companies (one of light infantry and one of rifles). During the conflict, a total of some 500 militiamen were embodied for active service, due to fears of naval incursions by the US fleet. The city of Halifax, the capital of Nova Scotia, also deployed one volunteer company of artillery. The general militia of New Brunswick was organized on county infantry battalions like that of Nova Scotia, albeit being smaller. In December 1812, to replace the local garrison of regulars that was transferred to mainland Canada, 500 militiamen were embodied for active service. Saint John, the colony's capital, had one company of volunteer artillery. In Newfoundland there were no militia units, only a volunteer corps known as the Loyal Volunteers of St John's, which comprised five infantry companies and was later renamed the St John's Volunteer Rangers. It was disbanded during the summer of 1814. Prince Edward Island had three infantry regiments of militia and three volunteer infantry companies in its capital city of Charlottetown. Each militia regiment was formed in one of the three counties that made up the colony, comprising a different number of battalions according to its population. The three volunteer companies of Charlottetown were named the Loyal Scottish Volunteers, Royal Kent Volunteers and Prince's Regent Volunteers. On Cape Breton Island, the local militia consisted of twenty infantry companies, each commanded by a captain and two lieutenants.

Following the end of hostilities with the USA, all the Canadian units of Select Militia and volunteers were disbanded, with the Sedentary Militia reorganized on forty-nine battalions in Lower Canada and thirty-one battalions in Upper Canada. These were not mustered for several years and did not see action until the outbreak of major rebellions on Canadian territory in 1837 and 1838. In November 1837, the Francophone population of Lower Canada rose up in revolt under the guidance of the *Parti Patriote*, or Patriot Party, that for several years had been asking for political reforms to increase the autonomy of the Canadian colonies and protect the rights of the Francophone community. The uprising did not involve large numbers of French-speaking Canadians and thus was suppressed quite easily by the British. The forces formed by the Patriots were defeated and their leaders were forced to flee to the USA as political exiles. The British authorities, however, soon realized that the Francophone rebels were merely reorganizing themselves in order to rise up again as soon as possible. After establishing their bases south of the border, the Patriots started gathering volunteers and weapons for a fresh insurrection. The British responded to these moves by deploying 5,000 soldiers on the territory of Lower Canada and creating a network of spies across the frontier with the USA. While these events took place in Lower Canada, the inhabitants of Upper Canada rose up in revolt too. The Anglophone settlers of the colony, like the Francophone ones of Lower Canada, asked the British government for a series of reforms that would favour the autonomy of their home territory as well as the reorganization of the local economy now that the fur trade was no longer so lucrative. As happened for Lower Canada, the British response to the requests of the Canadians was not a positive one, and subsequent malcontent caused an uprising. The initial revolt in Upper Canada was crushed quite rapidly and effectively by the British, but it soon became apparent that a larger rebellion was in the air, with the insurgents of Upper Canada collaborating with French-speaking rebels. In December 1837, the Canadian rebels established a base on Navy Island, a small inhabited island in the Ontario River on the border between Canadian Ontario and the US state of New York. The insurgents proclaimed the birth of a new state known as the Republic of Canada and continued their campaign against the British government by operating as pirates on Lake Erie and Lake Ontario. The republican leaders hoped that the USA would support them, but this did not happen. Indeed, the US authorities collaborated with the British, intercepting any convoy of supplies directed towards the Canadians. Having suffered a series of setbacks, the rebels changed strategy and restructured as a secret organization known as the *Frères Chasseurs*, or Hunters' Lodge. They conducted a series of raids and incursions from their bases in the USA, killing several people and causing significant material damage. In December 1838, the Canadian insurgents launched an invasion of Upper Canada, assembling a contingent of 400 men who marched on the city of Windsor. Here, however, they were utterly defeated by a British military force that was supported by some US elements. The Battle of Windsor marked a turning point in what became known as the Patriot War, proving to the Canadian population that the use of force would have not lead to positive results for their cause. By the beginning of 1839, the British government had despatched more than 10,000 regular soldiers to Canada to prevent the expansion of the rebellion, and soon after the Battle of Windsor, the Patriot War

Private (left) and officer (right) of the militia of New Brunswick in 1862. (*ASKB Military Collection*)

Private (left) and officer (right) of the militia of Nova Scotia in 1860. (*ASKB Military Collection*)

came to an end in both Lower and Upper Canada. Nevertheless, the bloody events of 1837–1838 convinced the British government that a series of reforms must be carried out in Canada in order to pacify the local population. 'Responsible government' (i.e. political autonomy) was granted to the Canadian colonies, whose financial problems were progressively resolved by the British government with substantial investments, mostly aimed at building new infrastructures. A diversification of economic activities began, together with an early form of industrialization. In 1840, with the Act of Union, Lower and Upper Canada were merged as the single Province of Canada with its own autonomous Parliament.

During the events of 1837–1838, the Canadian Militia was fully mobilized to support the British regulars in their counter-insurgency activities. In addition, thousands of volunteers who were not part of the militia enlisted and formed a multitude of short-lived corps. The militia of Lower Canada retained its peculiar organization dating back to the French colonial period with no modifications, while from 1829, that of Upper Canada started to be organized on infantry regiments with two battalions each. The first of these battalions consisted of men not older than 40 years of age, while the second, known as the Reserve Battalion, comprised older individuals. The first battalion mustered eight companies of light infantry, two of which were equipped with rifled muskets. In December 1837, the volunteer units formed in Montreal were assembled together in order to form three brigades: the first brigade consisted of the Montreal Rifle Corps (three companies of light infantry), Royal Montreal Cavalry (three troops of light cavalry) and one company of artillery; the second comprised the Montreal Light Infantry (six companies, one of which was made up of Scottish colonists) and Queen's Light Dragoons (one troop); and the third included three line infantry battalions of the Ward Associations (with ten companies each). Upon the outbreak of the insurgence, most of the regular British troops garrisoning Québec left the city, except for one company of artillery. Consequently, during early 1838, several corps of volunteers were formed in the city to replace the regulars. An infantry regiment with ten companies, known as the Royal Québec Volunteers, was formed, together with several other corps: the Québec Light Infantry with five companies, the Queen's Own Light Infantry of Québec with one company, one company of Scottish Highland infantry, one troop of cavalry, one artillery corps with eight companies, two companies of engineers, one company of artificers and two companies of sailors. These units were largely recruited from labourers, mechanics, tradesmen and merchants. By the beginning of 1840, all the militia and volunteer units of Lower Canada had been disbanded, except for a few militia corps that had been Embodied: one regiment of infantry – the 1st Provincial Regiment, with ten companies that were later reduced to four

Officer and private of the King's Royal Rifle Corps in the early 1870s. (*ASKB Military Collection*)

– and four independent companies of infantry that were tasked with guarding the frontier. After mobilization, the militia of Upper Canada was assembled into twelve Provisional Battalions that were attached to British regular units, but these were later consolidated into five Embodied Battalions whose members served full-time.

The city of Toronto, capital of Upper Canada, did not have a garrison of regulars when the revolution erupted, but two volunteer companies known as City Guards were raised from its citizens in December 1837. These were soon supplemented by two battalions of volunteers, known as the Queen's Rangers and Queen's Light Infantry. A small volunteer detachment was also formed to guard the Bank of Upper Canada in Toronto. In the Niagara region, to guard the border from US incursions, a corps of eight companies – the Queen's Niagara Fencibles – was raised. With the progression

Officer of the King's Royal Rifle Corps in 1870, wearing the peculiar campaign uniform and equipment that were used in Canada during cold months (including snowshoes). (*Colour plate by Patricio Greve Moller, copyright of Gabriele Esposito*)

of time, the militia was significantly enlarged, with the addition of several units to the infantry battalions mentioned above: twelve independent infantry companies, one rifle company, six cavalry troops and one artillery company. Around mid-1839, most of the militia and volunteer corps were disbanded, apart from a few Incorporated (i.e. Embodied) ones that were retained in service: five battalions of militia line infantry, one company of frontier infantry, one company of light infantry (the Glengarry Light Infantry Company), one troop of light dragoons, three troops of volunteer cavalry and one company of artillery. The single company of frontier infantry formed to guard the border in Niagara was also known as the Coloured Company because all its members were free blacks. Following the Act of Union of 1840, the few Embodied militia corps that still existed in Lower and Upper Canada were progressively disbanded. By 1843, only the Coloured Company of Niagara and the three troops of volunteer cavalry (two troops of the Royal Montreal Cavalry and one of the Queen's Light Dragoons) remained in service, the others having been disbanded in 1850. Following the formation of the Province of Canada, there were no serious attempts to reorganize and modernize the militia, except for the fact that the militia of Lower Canada started to comprise Reserve Battalions made up of men aged over 40. The various militia corps were mustered only rarely and thus lost most of their efficiency. Meanwhile, the volunteer corps became increasingly popular, the period 1840–1850 witnessing the formation of several new such units. The Canadian volunteer corps had three main categories: rifle units, cavalry units and artillery units.

The first volunteer unit of rifles to be formed in Canada after 1815 was the Québec Volunteer Rifle Company, which was raised in 1823. It was soon followed, in 1824, by the Montreal Volunteer Rifle Company, while the Toronto Rifle Company was organized in Upper Canada in 1834. All these units were armed with excellent rifled carbines – such as the British Army's Baker rifle – and were dressed in dark green like the King's Royal Rifle Corps. The Québec Volunteer Rifle Company did not have a very long history, while the Montreal Volunteer Rifle Company was expanded and became a battalion before being disbanded in 1854. The Toronto Rifle Company was not the only rifle corps of Upper Canada, several of the region's militia battalions having a volunteer company of riflemen attached. In 1854, a new volunteer rifle company, the Montreal Rifle Rangers, was formed in Lower Canada. During the War of 1812 against the USA, the Canadian military had included several volunteer corps of cavalry. These, like all the other volunteer units, were disbanded at the end of hostilities. In 1823 and 1824, two such corps, the Québec Volunteer Cavalry and Royal Montreal Cavalry, were reorganized. These were dressed and equipped like the contemporary British light dragoons, as Canadian territory – being mostly covered with dense woods – was not well suited to heavy cavalry. After 1824, several

Private (left) and NCOs (right) of the King's Royal Rifle Corps in the early 1870s. One of the NCOs wears the shell jacket that was used inside the barracks. (*ASKB Military Collection*)

battalions of Lower Canada's militia started to have an attached troop of volunteer cavalry. The same happened in Upper Canada, where several troops of volunteer cavalry were created. All these units were made up of wealthy gentlemen who wanted to serve with the militia but in a more 'aristocratic' fashion. They spent large

Officer (left) and NCO (right) of the Canadian Militia's line infantry in 1866, wearing the parade dress with shako. (*ASKB Military Collection*)

sums of money to buy the best horses available and to have very elegant uniforms. Following the outbreak of civil disturbances in 1837, the colonial government of Lower Canada mobilized the Royal Montreal Cavalry (with three troops) and formed the new Queen's Light Dragoons (which had one troop). These were soon supplemented by several short-lived troops of volunteer cavalry, which had little combat capability and were all disbanded at the end of hostilities. After 1843, as we have seen, the Royal Montreal Cavalry and Queen's Light Dragoons were retained in service and became collectively known as Provincial Cavalry. This unit's task, until its disbandment in 1850, was to guard the frontier with the USA south of Montreal. Upper Canada had its own volunteer cavalry units in 1837 and 1838, one of which – the Troop of Incorporated Dragoons – became Embodied and was retained in service for some time after 1839. In 1838, to prevent the recurrence of rebellions, a new mounted corps was raised in Lower Canada: the Rural Police, which comprised twenty-three independent small detachments tasked with patrolling the countryside. This was disbanded at the end of 1842, when Lower Canada had been completely pacified. Between 1840 and 1855, several volunteer troops of cavalry existed in both Lower Canada and Upper Canada, receiving no funds from the government and continuing to consist of well-to-do gentlemen. Regarding volunteer artillery, before the events of 1837–1838, Lower Canada had one company in Québec and another in Montreal. Upper Canada, meanwhile, had several companies of volunteer artillery attached to the various battalions of militia infantry. During the mobilization of 1837–1838, a new volunteer artillery corps – the Queen's Marine Artillery – was formed at Kingston in Upper Canada, with four companies of fifty men each. Its name derived from the fact that several of its officers came from the Royal Navy. In Lower Canada, one large artillery corps, with eight companies, was raised. Upon the end of hostilities, most of the volunteer artillery units in Canada were disbanded. The British authorities never had a high opinion of the volunteer artillerymen, since specific technical competences were needed for handling explosives and shooting field guns without causing incidents or damage to the civilian population.

The union of Lower Canada with Upper Canada in 1840 resulted in the formation of a combined Sedentary Militia of 426 battalions. However, this was merely a paper army based on the principle of universal service, with units mustering annually for only one day, and thus had very little formal training. This less than ideal situation, as has been seen, prompted some of the more patriotic and military-minded citizens to form various volunteer corps. Receiving no support from the government, these volunteer units provided their own uniforms and equipment. In 1846, a Militia Act was enacted in Canada, but did very little to change the existing situation. All able-bodied Canadian men aged between 18 and 60 were now liable to be called for service in the militia. They were divided into two classes according to their age: the first, comprising individuals aged 18–40, was to be mobilized first in case of need; the second, containing those aged 40–60, would be mobilized only in case of emergency. The Militia Act of 1846 also provided for a fast-assembling force of up to 30,000 men from the Sedentary Militia through voluntary enlistment or ballot in the event that fixed quotas were not met. In addition, for the first time, the act empowered the Governor General of Canada to order the formation of volunteer corps in case of need. By 1850, Canada thus remained almost wholly dependent upon British regular troops for defence.

With the outbreak of the Crimean War in 1854, the British government was obliged to draw upon its colonial garrisons in order to assemble an army to fight against Russia. By October 1854, almost all the British regular units stationed in Canada had left the country, with just three remaining behind: the 16th Regiment of Foot, the Royal Canadian Rifle Regiment and two companies of the Royal Artillery. The Royal Canadian Rifle Regiment had a quite peculiar history. It was formed in 1840 from veterans of the British Army serving in Canada who already had at least fifteen years of service. These men were given double pay (two shillings per day) and were also offered the prospect of a pension upon completion of twenty-one years of military service, as well as free grants of land upon retirement. The Royal Canadian Rifle Regiment was designed from the beginning as a light infantry frontier force, tasked with guarding the southern border of Canada. It consisted of ten companies divided into several small detachments that were spread out from Newfoundland in the east to Winnipeg (Manitoba) in the west. The Royal Canadian Rifle Regiment had a lot in common with the King's Royal Rifle Corps, being a unit armed with rifled carbines whose members wore the same dark green uniforms. Being elite riflemen trained to fight in the North American forests, the soldiers of the regiment enjoyed a high reputation. The Royal Canadian Rifle Regiment, however, had also been created to prevent desertions from the British line infantry regiments serving in Canada, as it offered good prospects to its members. In 1862, the Royal Canadian Rifle Regiment absorbed three independent companies of regular line infantry that had been formed in 1824, which were known as Royal Newfoundland Companies. These were mostly made up of former servicemen who were ex-patients of the Royal Hospital for Invalid Soldiers of Chelsea. These veterans were tasked with garrisoning the island of Newfoundland. The Royal Canadian Rifle Regiment continued to exist until 30 September 1870, always remaining one of the most important regular military units stationed in Canada.

In 1851, following the success of the Royal Canadian Rifle Regiment, the British government tried to settle 600 veterans (known as Enrolled Pensioners) in Canada,

Line infantryman (left) and rifleman (right) of the Canadian Militia in 1866, wearing the campaign dress with pillbox cap. (*Colour plate by Patricio Greve Moller, copyright of Gabriele Esposito*)

Uniforms of the Canadian Militia's garrison artillery in 1868, from left to right: officer in parade dress, NCO in campaign dress and NCO in stable dress. The uniforms are almost identical to those worn by the contemporary Royal Artillery. (*ASKB Military Collection*)

aiming to transform them into military colonists who could provide limited garrison services. The project, however, was not a great success due to the lack of land properties that could be assigned to the veterans, and it was finally abandoned in 1858. The military emergency caused by the Crimean War led to a new Militia Act in 1855, which contained a series of important innovations. According to the act, the Province of Canada was divided into eighteen military districts: nine in Lower Canada and nine in Upper Canada. The Sedentary Militia was retained, but a new Active Militia consisting of not more than 5,000 volunteers was created. This was to be armed, equipped, trained and paid by the colonial government. The volunteers of the Active Militia trained for ten days every year (twenty days for the artillerymen) and were paid at a rate of five shillings per day. The Active Militia consisted of fifty companies of rifles, sixteen troops of cavalry, five companies of foot artillery, seven companies of horse artillery and a small corps of provincial marines. In essence, the new Active Militia provided for a cadre of well-trained and well-armed volunteers who could be called upon to maintain internal security in the absence of British regular troops. The new Active Militia – whose units were defined as Class A – were so popular that by 1856, additional corps were authorized. These, defined as Class B, were trained and equipped by the Canadian government, but not paid. The Indian Mutiny of 1857 engendered widespread Canadian support for the motherland, which led the British government to plan the raising of a regiment of regulars from Canada for service in India. The new unit, the 100th 'Royal Canadian' Regiment of Foot, was formed in 1858 from volunteers (many of whom were members of the Active Militia). The regiment sailed to England and became part of the British Army, but recruiting for it in North America soon ceased and the unit thus lost its Canadian identity in all but name.

Following the outbreak of the US Civil War in 1861, the British government paid special attention to the defence of its territories in North America. This meant sending around 8,000 regulars to Canada as well as mobilizing the local militia for long periods. Thanks to the border tensions deriving from the Civil War, the Canadian Militia improved its standards of service, for example by assembling its independent rifle companies into battalions. The first of these had been formed in 1859 and was known as the 1st Battalion Volunteer Militia Rifles of Canada, which is still part of the Canadian Army today as the elite Canadian Grenadier Guards. Throughout the duration of the Civil War (1861–1865), several new battalions were formed by following the example of this first one. From 1860, several companies of the Canadian Militia started to be dressed in Highland style, which was quite popular in some areas (especially in Upper Canada), although these companies had the same organization and combat capabilities as the ordinary rifle units. Continuing the Canadian light infantry tradition, most of the rifle companies were dressed in dark green, but the militia cavalry was attired in light dragoon fashion. Diplomatic relations between Britain and the USA progressively worsened from 1861, largely because the British government provided significant support – in the form of bank loans and supplies of weapons – to the secessionist southern states of the Confederacy.

Consequently, it seemed plausible to many contemporary observers that hostilities could soon break out along the vast frontier that separated British Canada from the USA. The British government responded to the new menace by sending large amounts of modern weapons to Canada – where they were distributed to the local militia – and significantly reinforcing the regular garrison. A special staff of military instructors was also sent to retrain the Canadian Militia. In 1862, to protect railroad lines located near the frontier, thirty-six rifle and artillery companies were gathered together to form a special Grand Trunk Railway Brigade. In 1863, two new Militia Acts were passed, which increased the numbers of the Canadian Militia to 30,000 men and established the first schools of instruction for militia officers. The distinction between Class A and Class B troops was abolished and the militia foot units were re-uniformed as line infantry.

By 1866, shortly before the formation of the Dominion of Canada, the Canadian Militia had been expanded to comprise sixty battalions of infantry, fifty-nine independent companies of infantry (not yet formed into battalions), twenty-two troops of cavalry, eight companies of field artillery, forty-one companies of garrison artillery (assembled into six brigades), three companies of engineers and seven companies of naval infantry. These became collectively known as the Canadian Volunteer Force, as during the previous five years they had lost most of their original militia status and could now be compared to a regular army. No sooner had the US Civil War drawn to a close than a new threat materialized south of the Canadian border: the Fenian Brotherhood, the American branch of the Irish Republican Army that was formed in New York City in 1858, which started preparing an invasion of Canada. The Fenians were a strong military organization which wanted to achieve the independence of Ireland by invading a portion of the British Empire (i.e. Canada). Most of them were battle-hardened veterans of the US Civil War with extensive combat experience, who had been part of the famous Irish Brigade that fought for the Union Army. The Fenians attempted two invasions of Canadian territory, the first in 1866 and the second in 1870. These were both repulsed by the Canadian Volunteer Force, which was supported by small numbers of British regulars. To operate against the Fenians, the Canadian and British forces were organized into temporary field brigades, each of which usually consisted of 1,000 Canadians and 500 British regulars plus fifty cavalrymen and 100 artillerymen.

It is important to note that until 1870, a large portion of what is present-day northern Canada was not administered directly by the British government but by the Hudson's Bay Company, which exerted a monopoly over all the commercial activities connected with the fur trade that took place in the Arctic regions of Canada. The territory controlled by the Hudson's Bay Company consisted of three autonomous

38 Queen Victoria's Colonial Troops, 1837–1901

Uniforms of the Canadian Grenadier Guards: NCO in 1878 (left) and NCO in 1905 (right). (*ASKB Military Collection*)

NCO of the Cavalry School Corps in the early 1880s, wearing shell jacket and pillbox cap. The overall appearance is very similar to that of the British Army's light dragoons. (*ASKB Military Collection*)

entities: Rupert's Land, North-Western Territory and British Columbia. These were garrisoned by just a few militia corps before becoming part of the Dominion of Canada. The North-Western Territory had a small militia unit at the Red River Settlement in Manitoba, which was formed in 1835. It was known as the Red River Volunteers and consisted of just sixty men. This small corps, acting as a constabulary in its home settlement that was inhabited by colonists from different areas of the world, was disbanded in 1838. In British Columbia, the first militia unit was raised in 1851 from French-speaking *voyageurs* (fur hunters and traders) who worked for the Hudson's Bay Company. The corps, known as the Victoria Voltigeurs, performed the duties of a rural police and comprised only twenty men. It was disbanded in 1858. From that year, the US government started to exert increasing pressure on the southern border of British Columbia, seeking to expand its territories at the expense of the Hudson's Bay Company. The British government responded by establishing a permanent regular garrison in British Columbia (consisting of Royal Marines and Royal Engineers) and creating a new base for the Pacific Squadron of the Royal Navy at Esquimalt. On 19 November 1858, British Columbia ceased to be under the jurisdiction of the Hudson's Bay Company and became a new colony of the British Crown. From 1861, some units of volunteer militiamen were formed in the colony: the Victoria Rifle Volunteer Corps, consisting of sixty-seven men; the Victoria Pioneer Rifle Corps, made up of sixty free blacks, the Vancouver Island Rifle Corps, comprising one rifle company and one artillery company; the New Westminster Volunteer Rifles, consisting of fifty-four men; the New Westminster Home Guard, numbering sixty men; and the Seymour Volunteer Artillery Company, made up of former Royal Engineers. All these units were quite short-lived, since British Columbia was annexed to the Dominion of Canada in 1871. Rupert's Land became part of Canada in 1868, being followed by the North-Western Territory in 1870. The acquisition of such vast territories caused significant military issues to the Canadian government, as they had to be properly defended from both external and internal threats.

The large northern territories that were annexed to the Dominion of Canada between 1868 and 1871 were mostly inhabited by native tribes and the Métis, the latter being individuals of mixed blood who – quite often – were Francophone. The Métis fur hunters and traders had been the backbone of the Hudson's Bay Company and had always lived similarly to the natives, with whom they had established friendly relations. The French-speaking fur hunters lived in a semi-nomadic way and were not used to recognizing the existence of any superior authority. As a consequence, when their home territories came under Canadian control, they initiated a long-lasting struggle for freedom. In 1870, the leader of the Métis, Louis Riel, established a provisional government in the northern territories with the objective of preserving their autonomy. Initially, the Canadian government tried to negotiate with the Métis, but when this became impossible, a sizeable military force had to be sent against them in what became known as the Red River Expedition of 1870. Two battalions of Canadian Militia marched against the rebels, together with seven companies of the King's Royal Rifle Corps and some detachments of the Royal Artillery and Royal Engineers. The expedition was a great success, ending the revolt without a single shot being fired. The Canadian troops – some 1,400 men – traversed 1,200 miles of forested wilderness in a short period of time and without the loss of a single

NCO of the Canadian Militia's cavalry (left) and drum-major of the Canadian Grenadier Guards (right) in the early 1880s. (*ASKB Military Collection*)

Officer of the Canadian Militia's cavalry in 1886. (*ASKB Military Collection*)

life. Riel fled to the USA as a political exile, while the Canadian authorities started organizing the garrison of the northern territories. This was an extremely important move, the Métis needing to be controlled by the central government to prevent the outbreak of further uprisings. Furthermore, US expansion south of the Canadian border was causing great trouble among the native tribes of the Western Plains. Several native groups, coming under increasing US pressure in Montana and Dakota, were moving north to enter Canada, where they hoped to live free according to their traditional lifestyle.

The foot units of the militia did not have the mobility to patrol the vast woodlands and plains of the north, so a new mounted force had to be created to perform this difficult task. This happened on 23 May 1873, when the famous North-West Mounted Police was formed. This new paramilitary force consisted of 300 men assembled into six troops, who were responsible for garrisoning a series of isolated outposts stretching from the Atlantic to the Pacific. The impact of the North-West Mounted Police's arrival was extremely significant for the lands of Western Canada. The policemen, who mostly came from Ontario, brought peace and order to areas of Canada that had always been extremely wild. They managed to avoid the outbreak of Indian wars comparable to those taking place in the USA without using violence, even after the warlike Sioux tribe entered Canadian territory as exiles following the bloody Battle of Little Big Horn in 1876. The Canadian policemen, nicknamed the Mounties, patrolled the prairies and learned how to deal with the natives, whom they treated well and helped with the supply of food. During these years, the buffalo almost disappeared from the Western Plains due to intensive culls by white hunters. This had catastrophic consequences for many native communities – such as the Sioux – whose traditional lifestyle centred on the hunting of buffaloes. The presence of the mounted policemen opened vast territories of Western Canada to the arrival of settlers, who soon started building new towns over an immense area that had never before been inhabited by white people. The coming of the railway and of thousands of colonists was perceived as a mortal threat by the Métis, who still had no political representation in Ottawa but could count on the support of the natives. In 1885, the Métis rose up in revolt again, once more under the guidance of Louis Riel, who had returned from the USA. They established a secessionist government at Batoche and attacked several detachments of the North-West Mounted Police in what became known as the North-West Rebellion. The Canadians responded by sending most of their troops north, which led to a rapid crushing of the revolt after the capture of Batoche and of Riel in May 1885. During the following years, the North-West Mounted Police were significantly enlarged and came to comprise 1,000 men (later reduced to 750), largely because gold deposits were discovered in the newly settled territories of Yukon and the Klondike. The Mounties enforced law among the miners and patrolled the border that separated Western Canada from Alaska, which had been US territory since 1867.

Uniforms of the North-West Mounted Police: NCO in 1873 (left) and officer in 1904 (right). The dress of this famous police corps, with the peculiar wide-brimmed hat, soon became iconic. (*Colour plate by Patricio Greve Moller, copyright of Gabriele Esposito*)

While these events took place in the north, Britain's Atlantic Colonies in North America continued – at least temporarily – to remain separated from the Dominion of Canada, and thus kept their own autonomous military forces, as listed below.

Nova Scotia: From 1815, the militia of Nova Scotia consisted of three infantry regiments from Halifax, eleven infantry regiments from the interior counties and three infantry regiments from Cape Breton Island. Most of the regiments had two battalions each, while a few had a single artillery company attached. In Halifax there were also one company of volunteer rifles and two companies of volunteer artillery. In 1859, following the advent of a volunteer movement in Great Britain and due to the state of decay of the local militia, several new volunteer corps were formed in Nova Scotia: the Halifax Engineers, Halifax City Guards, Victoria Rifles, Scottish Rifles, Chebucto Greys, Mayflower Rifles, Halifax Rifles, Irish Volunteer Rifles, Dartmouth Rifles and Dartmouth Engineers. Most of these units were quite short-lived, while others were assembled together in May 1860 to form a single battalion with six companies that was stationed in Halifax. In 1866, a single cavalry troop, known as the King's County Guides, was created as part of the militia. During the same year, a Nova Scotia Naval Brigade was formed with seventeen companies of naval infantry. On 1 July 1867, Nova Scotia became part of the Dominion of Canada.

New Brunswick: After 1815, the militia of New Brunswick consisted of county regiments, several of which had a cavalry troop or an artillery company attached. Some militia regiments also had a company of sappers, which was made up of free blacks. From 1831, there were also two companies of Sea Fencibles in New Brunswick, which acted as a naval infantry corps tasked with performing garrison duties. In February 1838, following the outbreak of major revolts in Lower and Upper Canada, the various artillery companies of the militia were assembled together in order to form a single regiment with ten companies, called the New Brunswick Regiment of Artillery. In 1846, the cavalry troops were similarly brought together to form a new corps known as the Queen's New Brunswick Rangers. In 1848, this was transformed into an infantry unit, while a new cavalry corps with eleven troops – the New Brunswick Regiment of Yeomanry Cavalry – was created. As happened in many other colonies of the Crown, 1859 and 1860 saw the formation of several new volunteer corps in New Brunswick as a consequence of the flourishing volunteer movement in Britain: the Havelock Rifle Company, Queen's Own Rifles Company, Pisarinco Rifles, Duke of Rothesay's Rifles, Saint John City Guards, Saint John Rifles Company, The Royals, Zouave Company and Victoria Rifles. In 1863, the militia of New Brunswick was completely reorganized, being divided into Class A and Class B units. Despite this, some units retained an autonomous status: the Queen's New Brunswick Rangers and four battalions from Saint John. During 1862 and 1863, a militia company of engineers and a volunteer battalion of infantry were formed in Saint John. On 1 July 1867, New Brunswick became part of the Dominion of Canada, with its two best military units – the New Brunswick Regiment of Yeomanry Cavalry with four troops and the New Brunswick Regiment of Artillery with five companies – being absorbed into the Canadian Militia forces.

Prince Edward Island: Prince Edward Island was the smallest British colony in North America and was very lightly populated. Its territory was organized on three counties, each of which deployed a number of militia battalions. Three troops of volunteer cavalry and one company of volunteer artillery were attached to the units of militia infantry. In 1831, the foot battalions were amalgamated into three county regiments: the Queen's County Regiment with five battalions, the King's County Regiment with three battalions and the Prince's County Regiment with four battalions. After the outbreak of the Crimean War, some new volunteer corps were raised, notably the Charlottetown City Guards and Saint Eleanor Rifles. In 1860, the volunteer units of Prince Edward Island consisted of sixteen rifle companies, one cavalry company and one artillery company. In 1862, these were amalgamated into a single brigade, the Prince Edward Island Volunteer Brigade, consisting of three county regiments. On 1 July 1873, Prince Edward Island became part of the Dominion of Canada.

Newfoundland: Although the large island of Newfoundland had a limited population at the beginning of the nineteenth century, its position made it strategically important. For this reason, from 1824, it was garrisoned by two independent companies of British regulars known as Royal Newfoundland Companies. In 1862, these were absorbed into the Royal Canadian Rifle Regiment but continued to garrison Newfoundland. The first volunteer corps of the colony, the St John's Volunteer Light Infantry, was formed in 1859, consisting of four companies and existing until 1872 when it was disbanded. Another volunteer unit, the Harbour Grace Rifle Corps, was created during the 1860s. From 1871, Newfoundland was garrisoned by a small paramilitary force known as the Newfoundland Constabulary, which comprised just eighty officers and men. This included a small detachment from 1886. Newfoundland became part of Canada only in 1949.

Following the departure of the last British regular troops in 1871, Canada became responsible for its own defence and thus created a Royal Military College to train officers as well as an arsenal for the production of ammunition. The first two regular Canadian military units were formed on 20 October 1871 and consisted of two artillery batteries, known as 'A' and 'B'. Battery A was to garrison Fort Henry in Kingston, while Battery B garrisoned the Québec Citadel. The two new corps also functioned as schools of gunnery for the artillerymen of the militia. Each of the two

Trooper of the Royal Canadian Dragoons in the late 1890s. (*ASKB Military Collection*)

companies/batteries had a mounted division that acted as field artillery and a foot division that acted as garrison artillery. In 1883, the two artillery corps were joined together to form a single unit, known as the Royal Regiment of Canadian Artillery. In 1893, this regiment was restructured on two companies of field artillery and

48 Queen Victoria's Colonial Troops, 1837–1901

two companies of garrison artillery. Despite the formation of a regiment of regular artillery, the militia artillery continued to exist after 1871. In 1885, it consisted of forty-two garrison companies, which were assembled into three battalions in 1893 (Halifax, Montreal and New Brunswick). In December 1895, the militia artillery was reorganized on five regiments: the Halifax Regiment with four companies, Montreal Regiment with three companies, New Brunswick Regiment with three companies, Prince Edward Island Regiment with three companies and British Columbia Regiment with three companies. The Québec and Levis Regiment, with three companies, was added to the existing ones in 1889. There were also some independent field batteries; there were seventeen of them in 1895. The regular Canadian cavalry originated in 1883 as the Cavalry School Corps, a training unit that was transformed into the Canadian Dragoons during 1892. In 1885, a School of Mounted Infantry was also created in Canada, which became the Canadian Mounted Rifle Corps in 1891 and was amalgamated with the Canadian Dragoons in 1892. The original Cavalry School Corps and School of Mounted Infantry had the numerical consistency of a

Private of the Canadian Militia's infantry in 1910. (*Colour plate by Patricio Greve Moller, copyright of Gabriele Esposito*)

troop, whereas the Canadian Dragoons and Canadian Mounted Rifle Corps each had one squadron. In 1893, after the two squadrons were assembled together, they received the new denomination of the Royal Canadian Dragoons. The militia cavalry continued to exist after 1871 and was progressively consolidated into eight regiments. One of these, the first, was the Governor General's Bodyguard. Until 1867, two cavalry units of the militia – known as the Governor General's Bodyguard for Lower Canada (formed in 1862) and Governor General's Bodyguard for Upper Canada (formed in 1856) – provided the mounted escort for the Governor General. In addition to the eight consolidated regiments, there were several independent troops of volunteer cavalry and some short-lived temporary corps that were formed for the campaign of 1885 against the Métis. These were recruited from ranchers and cowboys, being designated as scouts or rangers due to their tactical functions. The first regular infantry unit was the Infantry School Corps formed in December 1883. This was progressively expanded and renamed the Canadian Regiment of Infantry (with one battalion) in 1892. The militia infantry continued to exist after 1871 and progressively adopted a structure based on regiments. Until the early years of the twentieth century, it numbered around 30,000 men.

The outbreak of the First Boer War in 1899 inspired thousands of Canadians to volunteer and serve under the Union Jack far from their homeland. A 2nd Battalion of the Canadian Regiment of Infantry was formed and sent to South Africa. This was followed by a brigade of field artillery and two battalions of mounted rifles. The former had three batteries, whose core was volunteer regulars from the two field companies of the Royal Regiment of Canadian Artillery. The battalions of mounted rifles had two squadrons each; the first battalion comprised many regulars from the Royal Canadian Dragoons, while the second included many members of the North-West Mounted Police. Another four battalions of Canadian Mounted Rifles were organized at a later date, but these arrived in South Africa when hostilities had already ended. The Canadians also sent a volunteer cavalry corps (not comprising any regulars) to fight against the Boers: Lord Strathcona's Horse Regiment, mustering three squadrons. Following the end of the Second Boer War, all these units were disbanded. In 1901, however, Lord Strathcona's Horse Regiment was re-raised. As a result of the above, in 1914, the Canadian regular forces comprised only four major units (in addition to the paramilitary North-West Mounted Police): the Canadian Regiment of Infantry, Royal Canadian Dragoons, Lord Strathcona's Horse Regiment and Royal Regiment of Canadian Artillery. A small engineer corps, consisting only of officers and NCOs, was formed in 1903 with the denomination of the Royal Canadian Engineers.

Chapter 2

West Indies

By the end of the eighteenth century, the Caribbean islands collectively known as the West Indies were one of the most profitable economic areas of the world. Having long been colonized by European powers, they produced large amounts of sugar that were sold around the globe at very high prices. In addition, albeit on a smaller scale, they produced other highly profitable crops such as indigo and coffee. Several of these islands were colonies of Great Britain, and alone represented about one-third of the country's foreign trade. The British West Indies comprised the following modern countries (some of which are still overseas territories of Britain today): the Bahamas, Barbados, Belize, Bermuda, Anguilla, Antigua and Barbuda, Virgin Islands, Dominica, Montserrat, Saint Kitts and Nevis, Grenada, Saint Lucia, Saint Vincent and the Grenadines, Cayman Islands, Guyana, Jamaica, Trinidad and Tobago, and Turks and Caicos Islands. Bermuda was part of the British West Indies administratively, but due to its geographical position in the Atlantic the maintenance of the military garrison was always the responsibility of Canada. Two of the territories listed above were not islands but larger colonies located on the Caribbean coastline of Central and South America: Belize (also known as British Honduras) and Guyana (British Guyana). British Honduras grew out of the Treaty of Versailles that was signed in 1783 at the end of the American Revolution, which gave Britain the right to cut logwood between the Hondo and Belize rivers in Spanish Central America. In 1786, the concession was expanded to include the area located between the Belize and Sibun rivers. In 1821, Central America became independent from Spain and thus Britain could exploit the politico-military weakness of the new nations bordering with Belize (notably Guatemala) to transform the existing concession into a proper colony. This happened in 1862, when the colony of British Honduras was officially created. Despite being quite small, Honduras was the location of several minor military campaigns fought by the British against the local native tribes of Mayas as well as of frequent border tensions with Guatemala. Guyana was seized by Britain from the Dutch during the Napoleonic Wars, although Britain had tried to occupy a portion of South American coastline located north of Brazil since the seventeenth century. Between 1814 and 1831, British Guyana consisted of three separate settlements, which had been established long ago by the Dutch: Essequibo, Berbice and Demerara. In 1831, these were unified as a single colonial entity, which flourished under British rule. Relations with the local natives were always quite positive, while relations with the bordering nations of South America (especially with Venezuela, which had been independent since 1830) were often quite tense. The western frontier of Guyana with Venezuela had never been properly defined, which became a serious problem during the late nineteenth century when large amounts of gold were discovered in the disputed area. Eventually, thanks to its political and military superiority, Britain annexed most of the disputed territories during the very last years of the century. Thanks to the direct taxes and duties from its Caribbean colonies, Britain was able to become the most important of the colonial powers during the eighteenth century, and it was absolutely vital for the Crown to protect such a lucrative portion of the ever-expanding British Empire. This became particularly true when, with the outbreak of the Revolutionary Wars, the British West Indies started to be menaced by the French (who also had their own flourishing colonies in the Caribbean). Operating in the West Indies, however, was not easy for the British Army. The local tropical climate was unsustainable for European troops, who were frequently decimated by terrible diseases such as tropical fevers. Consequently, British soldiers preferred avoiding service in the West Indies due to the unhealthy living conditions. To solve this problem and garrison the Crown's possessions

Private of the West India Regiments in 1815. Each regiment had a different facing colour and green was the distinctive one of the 5th Regiment.

Private from the Light Company of the 2nd West India Regiment in 1835. (*Colour plate by Patricio Greve Moller, copyright of Gabriele Esposito*)

in that part of the world, the British Army had no choice but to raise an increasing number of military units from the local communities of free blacks (although the slave trade was abolished in British territories only in 1807). The black soldiers, accustomed to the climate and temperatures of the Caribbean, could more easily live in the theatre of operations.

Until 1793, the British garrison of the West Indies was entirely made up of white regular regiments, which were sent to the Caribbean for periods of service before being transferred to other areas of the Empire. A single local unit existed, the Carolina Corps, which consisted of 300 American Loyalist blacks (former slaves) who had abandoned the Thirteen Colonies in 1779 and had been resettled by the British authorities in the West Indies. Many of these came from the Carolinas, hence the unit's name. In October 1793, the first of several new 'black' units was formed, the Corps of Black Military Artificers and Pioneers. Mostly recruited from ex-criminals who had been freed, it comprised 300 pioneers and 100 artificers. This unit was followed by several others, which usually bore the denomination of 'rangers' and had a distinct light infantry character. Many of these were originally raised by royalist French officers who had joined the British cause after the outbreak of the French Revolution; they usually each consisted of 200–300 soldiers and their members had some experience of jungle fighting. These ranger corps were soon supplemented by some garrison units created for static defence, but all these early black units had a distinctive temporary character and only a semi-regular status. This chaotic situation came to an end in 1795, when the British authorities finally decided to raise regular West India Regiments from the free blacks living in their Caribbean colonies. In 1795, the first eight of such units was created, which had white officers and NCOs. A single regiment consisted of one battalion, with ten companies (eight centre and two flank companies). By 1798, recruiting operations had been completed for all regiments and the following units had been formed:

- 1st West India Regiment (Whyte's)
- 2nd West India Regiment (Myer's)
- 3rd West India Regiment (Keppel's)
- 4th West India Regiment (Nicolls')
- 5th West India Regiment (Howe's)
- 6th West India Regiment (Whitelocke's)
- 7th West India Regiment (Lewes'), disbanded in 1802
- 8th West India Regiment (Skerret's), disbanded in 1802

These regiments soon proved to be excellent units, being employed with success against the French as well as to deal with slave uprisings, which were quite frequent in

Private of the 1st West India Regiment in 1873, wearing the summer campaign dress that was used during the Third Anglo-Ashanti War. (*Colour plate by Patricio Greve Moller, copyright of Gabriele Esposito*)

NCOs and privates of the 1st West India Regiment inspected by one of their British officers in 1885.

the Caribbean plantations. Most of the British West Indies were covered by jungles, where the 'maroons' (runaway slaves) created their own autonomous communities after fleeing from colonial plantations. Countering the insurgent and guerrilla activities of the maroons was one of the West India Regiments' most important tasks, since – at least on paper – the runaway slaves could gain the independence of their home islands, as had happened in Haiti, which became independent from France in 1804 after a bloody revolution. In 1798, to deal with this situation, another four West India Regiments were recruited:

- 9th West India Regiment, renumbered as the 7th West India Regiment in 1802
- 10th West India Regiment, renumbered as the 8th West India Regiment in 1802
- 11th West India Regiment, disbanded in 1803
- 12th West India Regiment, disbanded in 1803

The West India Regiments absorbed all the existing temporary infantry units of free blacks, including the Carolina Corps. In order to maintain the original establishments of the various regiments, an increasing number of slaves were bought by the British authorities and then freed to became part of the various units. These had detachments on all the islands that made up the British West Indies and thus performed some very important garrison roles. The West India Regiments served with distinction during the Napoleonic Wars, and two of them (the 1st and the 5th) participated in the Battle of New Orleans against the USA in 1815. Due to the success of the West India Regiments, the British authorities also decided to raise two units of Colonial Marines (naval infantrymen) during the Napoleonic Wars that were made up of free blacks. The First Corps of Colonial Marines (150 men) existed from 1808–1810, while a Second Corps of Colonial Marines (three companies, gradually expanded to six) was active between 1814 and 1816. Since most of the white Royal Marines were involved in military operations taking place in Europe against Napoleon, the Royal Navy badly needed some local naval infantry troops for service in the Caribbean. The 9th West India Regiment and 10th West India Regiment – which had been renumbered in 1802 – were both disbanded in 1815 when hostilities with both France and the USA came to an end. The demobilization of the West India Regiments continued during subsequent years: the 5th Regiment and 6th Regiment were dissolved in 1817, followed by the 3rd Regiment and 4th Regiment in 1819. The remaining two units – the 1st Regiment, mostly recruited from Jamaica, and 2nd Regiment, with most of its recruits from Barbados – remained a very important component of the British colonial military forces for most of the nineteenth century. Once the British West Indies ceased to be threatened by any foreign power, the West India Regiments were tasked with providing military contingents to operate in the British colonies of West Africa. The unhealthy tropical climate of this region was very similar to that of the Caribbean islands, and was thus unsustainable for Britain's white soldiers. From 1812, the West India Regiments had a recruiting station in West Africa, and after 1818 they started to provide detachments for service in that part of the British Empire. The soldiers of the West India Regiments effectively garrisoned British West Africa and participated with distinction in the local conflicts known as the Ashanti Wars (covered in detail in one of the following chapters). In 1840, the 3rd West India Regiment was re-raised by assembling together the Royal African Colonial Light Infantry (a colonial unit from West Africa, see one of the following chapters for more details) and three supernumerary companies of the 1st West India Regiment. The new unit was disbanded in 1870 and re-raised in 1897, before being dissolved permanently during 1904. The 4th West India Regiment and 5th West India Regiment were both re-raised in 1862 following the outbreak of the US Civil War, being disbanded in 1869. Curiously, during the period from 1856–1900, each of the existing regiments had an attached company of artillery. In 1888, the 1st West India Regiment and 2nd West India Regiment became, respectively, the 1st Battalion and 2nd Battalion of a unified West India Regiment.

The various British colonies in the West Indies also had their local units of militia, which were made up of all the able-bodied white colonists living there as well as the free blacks who were available for military service. Generally speaking, the white settlers served in cavalry units or as officers for infantry units, while the free blacks made up the rank-and-file of

Private of the 1st West India Regiment in 1885. As is clear from this picture, the uniform adopted by the West India Regiments from 1865 had an exotic cut, modelled on the dress worn by the Zouaves of the French Army. (*ASKB Military Collection*)

the foot units. The militiamen were required to provide their own uniforms and personal equipment, and they had to train on a regular basis, at least once every month. In case of emergency, the militia could be augmented with the inclusion of slaves, but these could not be issued with firearms (they could receive only pikes). All the British militias organized in the Caribbean also acted as constabulary forces to deal with slave uprisings. One of their primary tasks was to chase maroons and thus keep order in the plantations. At the end of the Napoleonic Wars, the British West Indies' militia corps were organized as follows:

Antigua: at the beginning of the nineteenth century, this colony's militia comprised several units, with two infantry regiments, one independent infantry company, one squadron of dragoons and one battalion of artillery. The two major infantry units were known as the Red Regiment and Blue Regiment, from the distinctive colour of their uniform's facings.

The Bahamas: each of the islands making up the Bahamas archipelago had its own militia units. Nassau had one infantry regiment with 500 men, one troop of light dragoons and one artillery company made up of volunteers. Crooked Island had one infantry and one artillery company, while Exuma and Long Island each had one infantry company.

Barbados: this colony had a large militia, comprising one infantry regiment for each of the eleven parishes that made up the territory of Barbados. In addition to these, which consisted of some 3,330 militiamen including 400 free blacks, there was a small cavalry unit of sixty troopers known as the Life Guards. Of the eleven infantry regiments, that organized in the parish of Bridgetown (the capital of Barbados) had an elite status and bore the name of the Royal Regiment of Militia.

Grenada: the militia of this island, mustering 1,200 men, consisted of five infantry regiments plus one troop of light dragoons and two companies of artillery. A smaller nearby island, part of the same colony, had its own independent infantry regiment.

Jamaica: this colony had the largest militia of all the British territories in the West Indies, which consisted of around 8,000 men and included at least 3,000 free blacks. These were organized in eighteen infantry regiments (one for each parish), three regiments of cavalry (one for each county, since each parish provided one or two troops) and eighteen artillery companies (one artillery company was attached to each infantry regiment). Over time, some independent rifle infantry companies were also established. Temporary companies were occasionally raised from local natives and loyal maroons, in order to counter the activities of the runaway slaves in the woods.

Saint Kitts: the militia of this colony comprised just two infantry regiments, known as the Windward Regiment and Leeward Regiment.

Saint Vincent: this British possession had two regiments and five independent companies of infantry, as well as one troop of cavalry and one company of artillery.

Tobago: in 1803, the militia of this colony was reorganized to comprise one infantry regiment with nine companies, one troop of cavalry and one company of artillery.

Trinidad: this British territory had a large and well-organized militia consisting of three regiments and eight independent companies of infantry, one regiment of light dragoons, one regiment of hussars, three corps of mounted chasseurs and one brigade of artillery. One of the infantry regiments – the Royal Trinidad Infantry – and the various cavalry units were all made up of white settlers, whereas the other corps mostly comprised free blacks who were under the orders of white officers.

British Guyana was garrisoned by detachments of the West India Regiments, to which it provided significant numbers of recruits. In addition, it had a 'burgher' militia made up of white settlers that the British inherited from the Dutch. This militia consisted of three separate branches, one for each of Guyana's main settlements: Essequibo,

NCO of the Guyana Police from the late 1890s.

Berbice and Demerara. In 1878, the autonomous militia corps were unified in order to form the new British Guyana Volunteer Force, which consisted of 340 men. In 1890, the last detachments of the West India Regiment left British Guyana, so in 1891 the colony had to reorganize its Volunteer Force into the new British Guyana Militia. The latter consisted of an Active Force, with better training and equipment, and a Reserve Force, that could be mobilized only in case of emergency. The Active Force was structured on one infantry battalion with seven companies and one artillery company. From 1839, British Guyana had a locally raised police force of 245 men, mostly recruited from the free blacks who were loyal to the colonial government. In 1891, this was partly militarized, being expanded in 1905 with the addition of a small mounted branch. Until 1866, British Honduras was garrisoned only by detachments of the West India Regiments. During that year, the first four companies of local volunteers were raised to fight against the natives, although these were soon disbanded. In 1885, a small detachment of paramilitary police was created, known as the British Honduras Constabulary Force. Nine years later, in 1897, the last detachments of the West India Regiment left British Honduras. As a result, in 1897, a single infantry company of volunteers – the Belize Light Infantry Volunteers – was formed for the defence of British Honduras. A company of volunteer mounted infantry was added to the existing corps in 1904, and the two units started to be known as the British Honduras Volunteer Force. The militia of Bermuda was largely neglected after 1815, despite the fact that the Royal Navy had an important base in the colony on Ireland Island. In 1894, a first volunteer unit was formed in the archipelago, the Bermuda Volunteer Rifle Corps, which consisted of three infantry companies. This was supplemented in 1895 by a single company of coastal artillery, the Bermuda Militia Artillery. Differently from the Bermuda Volunteer Rifle Corps, this also included black soldiers. Soon after its formation it was expanded and came to comprise two companies.

Chapter 3

Australia

In 1787, the famous First Fleet departed from Portsmouth to found a penal colony in Australia. This was the first permanent settlement of the new British colony, which had been discovered by James Cook only in 1770 and only became important for the Crown after the Thirteen Colonies were lost following the American Revolution. To guard the convicts transported on the First Fleet and to garrison the future penal colony, a unit known as the New South Wales Marine Corps was formed. This contained 160 Royal Marines (organized into four companies) who volunteered for service in Australia, a territory known at that time as New South Wales. The New South Wales Marine Corps acted as the garrison of Australia until 1791–1792, when the New South Wales Corps was formed. The latter started to be raised in Britain in 1789 as a regular infantry unit to make up the permanent garrison of New South Wales. It initially consisted of just 300 soldiers assembled into three companies, this very small establishment being explained by the fact that very few British soldiers were willing to serve in such a distant and little-known colonial outpost as Australia. After arriving in New South Wales, the corps was expanded to four companies through the enlistment of 100 former members of the New South Wales Marine Corps who had decided to remain in Australia. The early colonization of New South Wales proved to be very difficult, with local agriculture struggling to flourish. In addition, there was a chronic shortage of coins, which soon led to the adoption of rum as the main medium of local trade. The officers of the New South Wales Corps were able to buy all the imported rum that reached their colony and then exchange it for goods or labour at very favourable rates. Consequently, their unit soon became known as The Rum Corps. In 1795, a new governor tried to limit these illegal practices, but his efforts met with very little success and the general situation of the colony failed to improve in any significant way. In 1801, a small cavalry corps was raised, known as the Governor's Bodyguard of Light Horse, comprising men with some riding capabilities from the New South Wales Corps. It consisted of just two NCOs and six troopers, who were tasked with providing an escort to the governor and with carrying his despatches across the colony. Between 1802and 1806, members of the Governor's Bodyguard of Light Horse were drawn from convicts who had been pardoned, but this was a short-lived experiment. In March 1804, a major revolt of Irish convicts – many of whom were rebels who had participated to the Irish Revolution of 1798 – erupted in New South Wales and threatened the town of Sydney, at that time a very small settlement. The New South Wales Corps reacted very rapidly and defeated the rebels at the Battle of Vinegar Hill. Four years later, the soldiers of the British garrison revolted against their own authorities, which were by then strong enough to punish all the crimes deriving from the illegal sale of rum. This Rum Rebellion had some success and led to the creation of a military government

Trooper of the New South Wales Mounted Police in 1832 (left) and trooper of the New South Wales Native Police in 1852 (right). (*Colour plate by Patricio Greve Moller, copyright of Gabriele Esposito*)

in New South Wales, which remained in place until 1810. In 1809, however, a new governor was sent to Australia, together with the 73rd Regiment of Foot, and order was gradually restored in the young colony. In 1810, the New South Wales Corps, which had been transformed into the regular 102nd Regiment of Foot in 1808, was recalled to Britain, although 100 veterans and invalids were retained in service for garrison duties in New South Wales. The regiment took part in some minor actions during the War of 1812 against the USA before the Napoleonic era came to an end. The new garrison of Australia comprised the 73rd Regiment of Foot until 1814, when it was replaced by the 46th Regiment of Foot. From 1814, the following regular units of the British Army garrisoned Australia:

- 46th Regiment of Foot, 1814–1818
- 48th Regiment of Foot, 1817–1824
- 3rd Regiment of Foot, 1823–1827
- 40th Regiment of Foot, 1824–1829
- 57th Regiment of Foot, 1825–1832
- 39th Regiment of Foot, 1827–1832
- 63rd Regiment of Foot, 1829–1833
- 17th Regiment of Foot, 1830–1836
- 4th Regiment of Foot, 1832–1837
- 50th Regiment of Foot, 1833–1841
- 21st Regiment of Foot, 1833–1839
- 28th Regiment of Foot, 1835–1842
- 80th Regiment of Foot, 1837–1844
- 51st Regiment of Foot, 1838–1846

Private of the New South Wales Rifle Volunteers in 1854. (*Colour plate by Patricio Greve Moller, copyright of Gabriele Esposito*)

- 96th Regiment of Foot, 1841–1848
- 99th Regiment of Foot, 1842–1856
- 58th Regiment of Foot, 1844–1847
- 11th Regiment of Foot, 1845–1857
- 65th Regiment of Foot, 1846–1849
- 40th Regiment of Foot, 1852–1860
- 12th Regiment of Foot, 1854–1861
- 77th Regiment of Foot, 1857–1858
- 50th Regiment of Foot, 1866–1869
- 14th Regiment of Foot, 1867–1870
- 18th Regiment of Foot, 1870

The 100 veterans and invalids of the New South Wales Corps that remained in service after 1810 were known as the Royal Veteran Corps of New South Wales, a unit that was disbanded only in 1835. The regular infantry corps listed above were supported, during the course of the nineteenth century, by companies of both the Royal Artillery and Royal Engineers. As no regular cavalry units of the British Army were ever sent to Australia, several of the foot regiments in the colony formed detachments of mounted infantry that could patrol its vast interior areas. These areas soon became quite dangerous for the peaceful new colonists from Britain, being inhabited by numerous Aboriginal groups as well as the 'bushrangers', escaped convicts who preferred to risk the considerable hazards of life in the Australian wilderness rather than endure penal authority. These, also known as absconders or bolters, lived savagely and perpetrated a series of crimes. Their living conditions were extremely harsh and they had very few food resources, as a result of which the bushrangers embraced a life of banditry by preying on frontier farmers. These farmers were free settlers who had been encouraged to move to Australia and had been leased land by the British government. Such individuals, nicknamed 'squatters', were given convict labour by the colonial authorities in order to develop their farms. For the colonial authorities, the only way to deal with the activities of the bushrangers and thus protect the squatters was to deploy mounted patrols that could operate in the bush. A first detachment of mounted infantry (twenty-five men) was formed within the 3rd Regiment of Foot. Due to its excellent mobility, this first experimental corps operated with great success and intercepted a large number of bushranger bands. This encouraged the colonial authorities to organize a first corps of New South Wales Mounted Police on 7 September 1825. This unit was soon expanded, and by 1830 it mustered 100 men. In 1821, the Governor's Bodyguard of Light Horse was expanded and came to have twelve troopers. It changed its name to the Mounted Orderlies in 1834

Australia 65

NCO (left) and gunner (right) of the New South Wales Volunteer Artillery in 1873.
The uniform is almost identical to that of the contemporary Royal Artillery, including busby cap.

and started to recruit from the New South Wales Mounted Police. Two years later, the Mounted Orderlies were absorbed into the New South Wales Mounted Police, which numbered 150 men (assembled into five divisions) by 1850. The New South Wales Mounted Police played a prominent role in the early British colonization of

NCO of the New South Wales Lancers in 1903 (left) and officer of the Australian Volunteer Horse in 1900 (right). The slouch hat was the typical headgear of the Australian mounted units. (*Colour plate by Patricio Greve Moller, copyright of Gabriele Esposito*)

Australia, contributing in a significant way to the progressive expansion of the early settlements. By including former convicts in its ranks and employing very harsh methods against the Aborigines, the mounted policemen were the first to regularly cross the Blue Mountains that barred the way inland from Sydney. This allowed a steady expansion into the open country located beyond Sydney Cove, which led to the creation of new colonial territories in addition to the original one of New South Wales. In 1825, the colony that later became known as Tasmania was created, being followed in 1829 by what became Western Australia. The colony of South Australia was formed in 1834, that of Victoria in 1851, Queensland in 1859 and Northern Territory in 1863.

In 1851, gold was discovered in New South Wales and Victoria, causing a massive gold rush that forever changed the nature of Australia. Between 1852 and 1860, many thousands of immigrants, mostly coming from Britain, moved to Australia in search of gold: they became known as 'diggers' and started to build new settlements, forging

Private of the infantry (left) and officer of the artillery (right) from Victoria in 1884.

the identity of the Australian nation. The presence of so many newcomers and the discovery of large amounts of gold led to a new generation of bushrangers, who earned a living as bandits around the newly built boom towns of the diggers. Social tensions rose rapidly, especially among the squatters and the new group of the 'selectors' – newly arrived settlers who were given small land properties by the colonial government and were required to live permanently upon them before they qualified for a permanent title. The daily life of the selectors was hard and impoverished, which brought these newcomers into conflict with the established and privileged squatters (who owned large ranches with massive herds and flocks). To protect the diggers from bandits and prevent clashes between selectors and squatters, the colonial authorities had no choice but to form new paramilitary police corps similar to the New South Wales Mounted Police. In 1852, the 40th Regiment of Foot, which was stationed in Australia, provided a mounted infantry detachment of 125 men. They were selected for gold-escort duty and were rearmed with carbines, providing outriders to the gold convoys that were despatched from the Victoria goldfields to Melbourne. From 1842, the New South Wales Mounted Police were supported by a similar paramilitary corps, which was recruited from the

NCO of the Victorian Horse Artillery in 1890. (*Colour plate by Patricio Greve Moller, copyright of Gabriele Esposito*)

Aborigines who were loyal to the Crown: the New South Wales Native Police. This unit initially consisted of sixty men (commanded by white officers) who had already been employed as trackers for their skill in bushcraft. Being mounted and armed with carbines, they could operate against both bushrangers and hostile natives. By 1854, the New South Wales Native Police had grown to consist of ten divisions, each with fifty men. The native policemen contributed to the defence of goldfields, but their main tasks were protecting the frontier areas of the white settlements from Aboriginal attacks and pursuing diggers who operated without a licence. From 1839, New South Wales also had a Border Police, which was organized into a number of autonomous sections deployed on the outskirts of the Aboriginal lands. This corps, whose sections each comprised ten men, was mostly recruited from convicts or ex-soldiers who had been transported to Australia due to crimes of military indiscipline. They were supplied with horses and weapons, but were not paid for their services. By the end of the 1840s, the Border Police had been completely replaced by the much more effective Native Police. In 1853, the magistrates operating in the goldfields of New South Wales were authorized to recruit uniformed constables, who became known as the Gold Fields Police. Their formation was a significant step towards the development of a civilian police force, as in 1862 the Police Regulation Act was implemented in New South Wales. According to this act, all the existing police units in Australia – including the new mounted police corps formed in Victoria during 1853 – lost their original paramilitary status and were put under the control of a single Inspector General. The following paragraphs detail the history and organization of the various military units that were formed in the Australian colonies during the nineteenth century.

New South Wales: Prior to 1854, no military units were raised from the population of Australia, the colony being garrisoned instead by British regular corps. This changed after the outbreak of the Crimean War, since there were fears that Australia could be attacked by warships of the Russian Navy. In 1854, the colonial government of New South Wales approved the formation of several volunteer military corps: one rifle regiment with six companies, one troop of cavalry and one company of artillery. The New South Wales Rifle Volunteers soon became an elite military organization, made up of wealthy gentlemen from Sydney. It was disbanded in 1860 and replaced by a new unit, the 1st Regiment of New South Wales Rifle Volunteers. This comprised eight companies (later increased to twenty) and performed a series of auxiliary duties, for example relieving British regular units from their usual garrison service. In 1868, a Volunteer Highland Brigade, dressed in Highland fashion, was raised in New South Wales due to the visit of the Duke of Edinburgh. Consisting of just two foot companies, the brigade was disbanded in 1878. The troop of volunteer cavalry raised in 1854, known as the Volunteer Troop of Mounted Rifles and consisting of forty men, continued to exist until 1884, albeit assuming the new name of the Yeomanry Cavalry Corps of New South Wales. In 1885, a new cavalry corps was raised, the Sydney Light Horse, which initially consisted of a single troop but soon expanded and was renamed the 1st New South Wales Regiment of Cavalry. The corps was converted into a lancer unit in 1891, becoming the New South Wales Lancers. Eight years later, one squadron of the regiment was sent to Britain for training. The company of volunteer artillery formed in 1854 was disbanded two years later, but three new companies of volunteer artillerymen were raised in New South Wales in 1859. By 1878 there were eight locally raised volunteer artillery companies in New South Wales.

By 1871, similarly to what happened in Canada with more or less the same timing, the withdrawal of British regular forces from New South Wales had been completed and the local volunteer forces thus assumed total responsibility for the defence of the colony. As a result of this important change, the local government decided to raise three companies of permanent regular troops: two of infantry and one of artillery. The two infantry companies were quite short-lived, being disbanded in 1873, but the artillery company (known as Field Battery A) was retained in service. In 1867, the volunteer infantry of the 1st Regiment of New South Wales Rifle Volunteers was reorganized on twenty-eight companies according to the Volunteer Regulation Act that was promulgated during that year. This also gave provision for land grants in recognition of five years of volunteer service. This new system did not work very well, with several members of the volunteer corps selling their land grants for profit rather than living on them by themselves. Consequently, land grants were soon replaced by partial payments. In 1876, a second company of permanent artillery was raised, being followed by another during 1877. A small Engineer Corps was also formed in 1877, with one company, later increased to two. In 1878, the infantry was restructured on three regiments, which were later increased to five. When news of the Dervish uprising in Sudan that led to the killing of General Charles Gordon reached Australia in 1885, the colonial government of New South Wales assembled an expeditionary force and offered its services to Britain. The expeditionary corps consisted of one infantry battalion and one artillery company, which were sent to Sudan but saw very little action in Africa. This was the first major campaign fought overseas by the Australian troops. The combat experiences in Sudan convinced the authorities of New South Wales to establish a School of Gunnery for the artillery in the colony and to expand the volunteer cavalry – as we have seen – with the formation of the 1st New South Wales Regiment of Cavalry. In 1885, four batteries of reserve artillery were created, but these were disbanded in 1892.

During 1888, a new regiment of mounted infantry, known as the New South Wales Mounted Infantry, was raised. This had five squadrons and was renamed the New South Wales Mounted Rifles in 1893. A small group of officers from New South Wales served with units of the British Army in India during 1894 in order to gain operational experience. In 1895, the infantry was expanded with the addition of two new regiments; another one was added in 1899. A new regiment of volunteer cavalry was formed in New South Wales in 1897 by gathering together the best cavalrymen in the colony. The new unit, the 1st Australian Volunteer Horse, comprised expert riders from the interior areas of New South Wales. The four squadrons of the new regiment soon acquired a solid reputation and were praised by contemporary British observers. The year 1897 also saw the formation of a Railway Volunteer Corps and a National Guard made up of veterans who had served in the various volunteer corps. Following the outbreak of the Second Boer War in 1899, New South Wales sent an expeditionary force to South Africa, followed by a second one in 1900. Both the expeditionary corps

Officer of the Victorian Mounted Rifles in 1893. (*Colour plate by Patricio Greve Moller, copyright of Gabriele Esposito*)

Private of the South Australian Volunteer Infantry in 1868. (*Colour plate by Patricio Greve Moller, copyright of Gabriele Esposito*)

were made up of volunteers from the military units in the colony. During the mobilization of 1900, two new regiments of mounted rifles were raised from bushmen: the New South Wales Citizens' Bushmen with four squadrons and New South Wales Imperial Bushmen with six squadrons. Both units served in South Africa and were disbanded in 1901. From 1863, New South Wales also had a Volunteer Naval Brigade with five naval infantry companies (which were raised by following the example of the colony of Victoria, which had two naval infantry companies from 1861). By 1902, the military forces of New South Wales consisted of eight regiments of infantry, the New South Wales Lancers, the New South Wales Mounted Rifles, the Australian Volunteer Horse, four companies of field artillery, six companies of garrison artillery and four companies of engineers.

Victoria: The first volunteer military forces of the colony of Victoria were raised following the outbreak of the Crimean War. They consisted of three corps: the Melbourne Volunteer Rifle Regiment (whose members underwent some artillery training), Geelong Rifle Corps and Volunteer Yeomanry Corps (a cavalry troop). In 1859, the Melbourne Volunteer Rifle Regiment was assigned an establishment with ten companies, the Geelong Rifle Corps having three companies. During that same year, three new battalions of volunteer infantry were formed, known as the North Battalion, South Battalion and Country Battalion, each of them having eight companies. The Melbourne Volunteer Rifle Regiment was later transformed into an artillery corps of eleven companies, bearing the denomination of the Royal Victorian Volunteer Artillery. The Ballarat Volunteer Rifle Regiment was formed in the Ballarat district in 1858. In 1870, two new foot units were raised from the city of Melbourne, the 1st Battalion Metropolitan Rifles and 2nd Battalion Metropolitan Rifles. In 1883 and 1884, all the volunteer infantry units of Victoria were disbanded and replaced by four battalions of militia infantry, which were later increased to five with the addition of a new corps known as the Victorian Rangers. As regards cavalry, several new troops of mounted volunteers were raised following the example of the Volunteer Yeomanry Corps. In 1862, these were assembled together to form the Victorian Volunteer Light Horse regiment. In 1885, this unit was disbanded, except for one troop that was later transformed into an independent squadron. A new cavalry unit was created in 1885, the Victorian Mounted Rifles, a regiment with nine companies. In 1891, these were reorganized as two battalions due to the distinct mounted infantry nature of the regiment (which deployed small

Private of the infantry from Southern Australia in 1890. (*Colour plate by Patricio Greve Moller, copyright of Gabriele Esposito*)

Trooper of the Queensland Mounted Infantry in 1896. (*Colour plate by Patricio Greve Moller, copyright of Gabriele Esposito*)

detachments in various locations of its home colony). Artillery consisted of the Royal Victorian Volunteer Artillery regiment, which from 1870 was supported by a single company of permanent regular artillery. In 1885, an independent battery equipped with machine guns was created; this was converted into a company of mounted artillery in 1889, which assumed the name of the Victorian Horse Artillery and continued to exist until 1897. By 1902, the military forces of Victoria consisted of the Victorian Infantry Brigade with five battalions, the Victorian Mounted Rifles, the Royal Victorian Volunteer Artillery, two companies of regular artillery and two companies of engineers.

South Australia: Following the outbreak of the Crimean War, several companies of volunteer infantry were formed in the colony of South Australia. In 1860, these were assembled together to create a single regiment of volunteer infantry, the Adelaide Regiment of Volunteer Rifles. This denomination was soon changed to the South Australian Volunteer Infantry. The corps was disbanded for some years during the early 1870s, but was re-raised on a permanent basis in 1877. In 1854, a single troop of South Australian Mounted Rifles was created, but this small cavalry unit was disbanded in 1856. During 1860 a new mounted troop, the Reedbeds Mounted Volunteers, was formed. In 1868, this became part of a newly raised cavalry unit, the South Australian Regiment of Volunteer Cavalry. This was disbanded in 1870 and re-raised in 1886 as the South Australian Volunteer Mounted Rifles. In 1877, another cavalry corps was formed in South Australia, the Adelaide Mounted Rifles, which was re-equipped with lances in 1886. By 1902, the military forces of South Australia consisted of two infantry regiments with two battalions each (the South Australian Volunteer Infantry and one militia regiment), the South Australian Volunteer Mounted Rifles (with seven squadrons), one company of field artillery and one company of garrison artillery.

Queensland: The first locally raised military units of this colony were formed in 1860, comprising two companies of infantry plus two of mounted rifles. By 1870, these had been expanded to consist of the Queensland Rifle Corps with ten companies and Queensland Mounted Rifle Corps with seven companies. In 1879, the Queensland Rifle Corps was divided into two regiments, each having four companies. The military forces of Queensland adopted a mixed nature in 1884, consisting of militia corps recruited from metropolitan areas and volunteer corps containing men from rural areas. The new militia infantry consisted of three regiments, exactly like the new volunteer infantry that mustered the following corps: the Queensland Volunteer Rifles, Queensland Scottish Volunteers and Queensland Irish Volunteers. Following the military reform of 1884, the Queensland Mounted Rifle Corps was restructured on eight companies, which were progressively augmented to twelve by 1893. In 1900, the unit became known as the Queensland Mounted Infantry and was restructured on four battalions. As for artillery, a small Volunteer Artillery Corps was formed in 1862, a second company being added to the unit four years later. In 1884, two new companies of regular artillery were created and the two existing ones were transformed into militia corps. By 1902, the forces of Queensland consisted of six regiments of infantry, the Queensland Mounted Infantry with four battalions, three companies of artillery and one company of engineers.

Tasmania: Between 1859 and 1863, several small volunteer corps of both infantry and artillery were formed in Tasmania. These, however, were quite short-lived and had all disappeared by 1867. As a result, the colonial authorities created just two companies of volunteer artillery, tasked with supporting the British regular units that garrisoned Tasmania. When the garrison left the colony in 1870, no local military forces existed in Tasmania except for the two artillery companies. In 1877, one infantry unit, the Tasmanian Volunteer Rifle Regiment, was created with six companies. From 1883, Tasmania also had a single company of engineers. By 1902, the military forces of Tasmania consisted of the Tasmanian Infantry Regiment (the former Tasmanian Volunteer Rifle Regiment) with three battalions, the recently formed Tasmanian Mounted Infantry with five troops, two companies of artillery and one company of engineers.

Western Australia: The first locally raised units of this colony were created in 1862, comprising two rifle companies plus one cavalry troop. In 1872, the infantry was reorganized as the Metropolitan Rifle Volunteers with six companies and a first troop of horse artillery was created. Two years later, a new foot battalion known as the Western Australian Volunteers was organized, while the mounted troops – which had assumed the denomination of the Western Australia Mounted Infantry – were progressively expanded to comprise four companies. In 1884, the infantry was restructured on five battalions: the Western Australian Volunteers, Metropolitan Rifle Volunteers, Albany Rifle Volunteers, Geraldton Rifle Volunteers and Fremantle Rifle Volunteers. In 1893, the artillery was reorganized as a single permanent battery, which was supplemented from 1899 by a volunteer company of garrison artillery. By 1902, the military forces of Western Australia comprised one infantry brigade with five battalions, the Western Australia Mounted Infantry regiment with four companies, two batteries of permanent artillery and one company of garrison artillery.

Australia 77

NCO of the infantry from Tasmania in 1899. (*Colour plate by Patricio Greve Moller, copyright of Gabriele Esposito*)

On 1 January 1901, the six Australian colonies federated together in order to form the Commonwealth of Australia, the first unified Australian nation. As a consequence of this political event, which increased Australia's autonomy from Britain, the forces described above were assembled together to form a single military organization. This process was not an easy one, since the various contingents were jealous of their independence. It was only in 1903 that a new military structure became effective. According to this, the Australian military would consist of three infantry brigades and six light horse brigades. Each infantry brigade was to muster four infantry regiments, for a total of twelve, numbered in progressive order. Attached to each infantry brigade would be three batteries of field artillery and one company of engineers. Each light horse brigade was to muster three mounted regiments, with a total of eighteen, again numbered in progressive order. Attached to each light horse brigade were to be one battery of field artillery and one section of engineers. These military units were collectively known as Field Forces, most of them comprising militiamen, with only the artillerymen and engineers being professional soldiers serving on a permanent basis. In addition to the Field Forces there were the auxiliary Garrison Troops, which consisted of volunteers with limited training; these were allocated

Officer of the infantry from Western Australia in 1900. (*Colour plate by Patricio Greve Moller, copyright of Gabriele Esposito*)

to each state of the new Commonwealth of Australia according to the number and size of fortifications that required manning. However, the general structure prescribed for the Field Forces in 1903 was never fully implemented and was changed in 1906. The number of infantry brigades was reduced to two and that of light horse brigades to four, while four mixed brigades of infantry and cavalry were formed. New South Wales provided the 1st Infantry Brigade, 1st Light Horse Brigade and 2nd Light Horse Brigade; Victoria provided 2nd Infantry Brigade, 3rd Light Horse Brigade and 4th Light Horse Brigade; the Queensland Brigade had two regiments of infantry and two squadrons of light horse; the South Australian Brigade had one regiment of infantry and two regiments of light horse; the Western Australian Brigade had one regiment of infantry and one regiment of light horse; and the Tasmanian Brigade had one regiment of infantry and one regiment of light horse. The mixed brigades were created because the smaller ex-colonies could not support a purely infantry or purely cavalry formation.

Chapter 4

New Zealand

The two major islands of New Zealand – South Island and North Island – were visited by James Cook in 1769. During the following years, they attracted an increasing number of European whaling or sealing vessels, with the first contacts between foreigners and the local Māori population taking place. The warlike Māori were quick to see the commercial advantages of trading with the whites and thus started exchanging flax for flintlock muskets. By the beginning of the nineteenth century, a number of small European coastal settlements had developed in New Zealand, which traded with the Māori and served as ports of call for passing ships. Such settlements were not controlled by any European colonial power, meaning their dealings with the Māori were unregulated. Nevertheless, they sold large numbers of modern firearms to the various Māori groups, which had enormous consequences for the latter's traditional society. Between 1820 and 1843, New Zealand was devastated by violent inter-tribal conflicts – fought with European weapons – that became known as the Musket Wars. At the beginning of the 1840s, the British, who by virtue of their Australian colonies considered New Zealand to be within their sphere of influence, decided to intervene in Māori tribal politics to limit the growing influence that France and the USA were establishing over New Zealand. A first major conflict – known as the Flagstaff War – was fought between Great Britain and the Māori from 1844–1846. This caused severe losses to the British, the warlike Māori fighting with enormous courage to preserve the independence of their homeland. Employing hit-and-run guerrilla tactics, the native warriors exploited the British Army's difficulties in operating on such a wild and inhospitable terrain as New Zealand. Most of the Māori were armed with modern weapons comparable to those used by the British and proved to be excellent marksmen. Each Māori tribal group also had strong fortifications on its territory. The outcome of the Flagstaff War was indecisive, and during the following decades the British had to continue fighting against the Māori in order to establish control over New Zealand. The Māori Wars came to an end only in 1872 after the last resistance of the natives had been crushed. Until 1841, New Zealand was not an independent administrative entity within the British Empire, and it was only in 1843 that the first British regular troops were

New Zealand 81

Trooper of New Zealand's militia cavalry in 1867. (*Colour plate by Patricio Greve Moller, copyright of Gabriele Esposito*)

Private of the Forest Rangers from New Zealand in 1865. (*Colour plate by Patricio Greve Moller, copyright of Gabriele Esposito*)

garrisoned there. The following units of the British Army were stationed in New Zealand during the period 1843–1870:

- 96th Regiment of Foot, 1843–1847
- 58th Regiment of Foot, 1845–1858
- 99th Regiment of Foot, 1845–1847
- 65th Regiment of Foot, 1846–1865

- 40th Regiment of Foot, 1860–1866
- 57th Regiment of Foot, 1860–1866
- 14th Regiment of Foot, 1860–1867
- 12th Regiment of Foot, 1860–1866
- 70th Regiment of Foot, 1863–1866
- 43rd Regiment of Foot, 1863–1866
- 50th Regiment of Foot, 1863–1866
- 18th Regiment of Foot, 1863–1870
- 68th Regiment of Foot, 1864–1866

These regular infantry corps were supported during the course of the nineteenth century by companies of the Royal Artillery and the Royal Engineers. No regular cavalry units of the British Army were ever sent to New Zealand. Due to the geographical isolation of the colony and the extremely warlike nature of the Māori, the political authorities of New Zealand soon made provision for creating a local militia, despite there being a limited population of white settlers. In 1845, a Militia Act imposed a duty for all able-bodied men aged 18–65 to have military training for twenty-eight days annually and to be available when called upon to serve in defence of their district. The first small detachments of militiamen were thus formed and started to perform a series of auxiliary duties for the British regulars (for example by acting as pioneers). In 1858, a further Militia Act provided the capability to raise units of volunteers, which unlike the militia could be called on to fight anywhere in New Zealand. One of the first volunteer corps to be raised was the Taranaki Rifles, which consisted of two light infantry companies and participated in several combat actions against the Māori. By 1860, several units of militia and volunteers had been created in New Zealand thanks to the steadily growing settler population. In 1865, the colonial government decided to reorganize its military forces in view of the upcoming withdrawal of British regulars from its territory (which was completed, like for Canada and Australia, by 1870). A new Volunteer Force was formed to replace the militia, whose members qualified for a remission from the price of any land purchased from the Crown after five years of service. The new Volunteer Force consisted of rifle companies, cavalry troops and artillery companies; there were no major units and the whole military organization was designed to perform local garrison duties. The volunteers were usually assigned land that had been confiscated from the Māori, according to a practice that had already started in 1846 when a number of former British regulars were settled around Auckland as military colonists and assumed the denomination of the Royal New Zealand Fencible Corps. These were armed and equipped like the ordinary militia corps and were disbanded in 1863.

New Zealand 83

Private of the New Zealand Armed Constabulary in 1870. The shawl-kilt was part of the Māori's traditional dress. (*Colour plate by Patricio Greve Moller, copyright of Gabriele Esposito*)

Trooper of New Zealand's Territorial Force cavalry in 1910.

During 1863, having already disbanded most of the existing volunteer corps, the colonial authorities of New Zealand created a new unit of Forest Rangers. These were formed specifically for the conducting of counter-guerrilla operations against the Māori and were trained for operating in the wild forests of New Zealand. The pay offered to members of the Forest Rangers was three times that of the militia, meaning the new corps enjoyed an elite status. It consisted of two companies, which specialized in patrolling the interior areas where both the British regulars and militia were disadvantaged due to their limited mobility. The Forest Rangers attacked Māori settlements and organized ambushes exactly like their opponents. They played a prominent role in the final pacification of the Māori communities before being disbanded in 1867.

By the end of 1867, with it appearing that the Māori Wars were coming to an end, the colonial government decided to establish a new corps of paramilitary police that could effectively patrol the recently pacified native territories. This was called the New Zealand Armed Constabulary and was organized on autonomous divisions, each of which ranged in size from a minimum of sixty to a maximum of 100 men. Two such divisions were raised from Māori warriors who were loyal to the Crown. The New Zealand Armed Constabulary also comprised a small artillery section and some mounted detachments, and was the first professional military force recruited in New Zealand. Between 1885 and 1887, due to the fear of a Russian naval attack, the Volunteer Force was reorganized; the rifle companies were assembled into battalions and the cavalry troops into regiments. At the same time, a first school of military instruction was established. During the closing decade of the nineteenth century, despite these measures, the Volunteer Force entered into a state of decay: its drill was out of date, its instructors were overworked and modern weapons were available only in small numbers. Consequently, the most inefficient corps of the Volunteer Force were disbanded by 1895 and the territory of New Zealand was restructured on five military districts. In 1909, a Defence Act came into force in New Zealand, which reduced the number of military districts to four and transformed the Volunteer Force into the new Territorial Force. The latter was the first form of permanent army ever raised in New Zealand, and by 1911 it consisted of sixteen infantry regiments (battalion-strength, with four for each district), twelve mounted rifle regiments (three for each district) and four artillery brigades (one for each district).

Chapter 5

South Africa

The first European settlement at the Cape of Good Hope was established by the Dutch East India Company in 1652, but for a long time the new colony on the extreme southern tip of Africa remained very small. The Dutch had only gone to the Cape to establish a way-station to service their fleet on the long haul to their flourishing colonies in Asia, and were not interested in exploring or settling the hinterland of present-day South Africa. This region was inhabited by some of the most warlike peoples of Africa, notably the Xhosa and the Zulu. Over time, the number of Dutch colonists in South Africa expanded significantly, mostly due to the arrival of religious refugees from Europe. These, similarly to the Puritans in the Thirteen Colonies, grew into a hardy breed that established flourishing farms thanks to the employment of slave labour and pushed with great determination for expansion into the African hinterland. The new colonists, who became known as Boers (farmers), were always in search of fresh hunting and grazing lands. They lived in a very austere and independent fashion, developing their own culture and traditions. The Boers defined themselves as Afrikaners (white Africans) and did not recognize the authority of the Dutch East India Company. By the end of the eighteenth century, European settlement had crept steadily along the eastern seaboard of South Africa and the Boers had come into conflict with the Xhosa. In 1806, as part of the Napoleonic Wars that saw the Dutch fighting as allies of France, Cape Colony was conquered by the British. The small settlement was located in a strategic position, controlling the most significant commercial and naval routes connecting the Atlantic Ocean with the Indian Ocean. By controlling it, the British could secure their lines of communication with India in an age before the construction of the Suez Canal. Most of the Boers living in the frontier areas of Cape Colony soon felt that the new British administration was unsympathetic to their needs, especially after it tried to outlaw slavery (which was the basis of the Boers' rural economy). In addition, the British did not look favourably at penetration into the lands of the Xhosa, as this caused the outbreak of bloody frontier wars. In 1835, the Boers commissioned reconnaissance parties to travel beyond the boundaries of Cape Colony in search of lands that might be opened up for white settlement, away from British control. Between 1836 and 1840, around 6,000 Boers packed their belongings into ox-wagons and migrated into the interior of South Africa in what became known as the Great Trek. These Boers were organized into groups linked by family ties and led by ambitious leaders. Their migration provoked decades of conflict with the native African groups they encountered along the way, which caused many problems for the British colonial authorities.

The Dutch East India Company had established a permanent military garrison at the Cape of Good Hope during the late eighteenth century. Initially, the Dutch organized a Corps of Bastard Hottentots, which was made up of local black recruits of mixed ancestry (half-white and half-Hottentot, or native nomadic pastoralists). This early unit, with 400 soldiers, was disbanded in 1782 after the French Pondichéry Regiment arrived at the Cape to garrison the colony. At the time, both the Netherlands and France were at war with Britain as part of the American Revolution. The French, worried that the Royal Navy might capture the Cape of Good Hope from their Dutch allies, sent one of their colonial regiments (originally raised for service in French India) to garrison the settlement. In 1786, after the French troops had left South Africa, the Dutch replaced them by recruiting a unit of German mercenaries. This force, due to the geographical provenience of its members, was known as the Württemberg Cape Regiment. Structured on ten companies, it was a very short-lived corps, serving in South Africa only until 1791. In 1793, the Dutch re-formed their Corps of Bastard Hottentots, which was given the new denomination of the Pandour Corps and numbered 200 men. In 1795, the British occupied for the first time – albeit

Private of the Cape Regiment in 1806. (*Colour plate by Patricio Greve Moller, copyright of Gabriele Esposito*)

NCO of the Cape Mounted Riflemen in 1835. (*ASKB Military Collection*)

only temporarily – the Cape of Good Hope, and during the following year they reorganized the Pandour Corps as the new Hottentot Corps, with 300 men. In 1801, this was expanded to become a regiment with ten companies, which was designated the Cape Regiment. Following the signing of the Peace of Amiens, the Cape of Good Hope was returned to the Dutch, who kept in service the Cape Regiment but twice changed its name during the following years (first to the Corps of Free Hottentots and then the Hottentot Light Infantry). In 1806, the British reoccupied

Officer of the Cape Mounted Riflemen in 1846, wearing the peaked cap used on campaign. (*Colour plate by Patricio Greve Moller, copyright of Gabriele Esposito*)

Boer irregular of the commandos. (*Colour plate by Patricio Greve Moller, copyright of Gabriele Esposito*)

the Cape of Good Hope for good and reorganized the Cape Regiment. This had ten companies, whose officers and NCOs were all whites, while the rankers were recruited from local blacks who had been loyal to the Dutch colonial authorities. The native South Africans were perfect as light infantrymen, being used to living and fighting in the wild bush of the region. The Cape Regiment was expanded with the addition of a light cavalry troop during the Napoleonic Wars. In 1817, however, most of the corps was disbanded and what remained of it was reorganized as two company-sized autonomous units tasked with protecting the north-eastern frontier of the Cape Colony: the Cape Light Infantry and Cape Cavalry. The latter was the former light cavalry troop of the Cape Regiment.

In 1820, these two small units were combined under a unified command and re-designated the Cape Corps. In 1827, its cavalry component was disbanded, while the infantry portion was expanded to become a battalion of mounted infantry that assumed the denomination of the Cape Mounted Riflemen. This was always fully horsed and armed as cavalry, despite being paid as infantry and operating as mounted infantry. By 1854, due to mutinous conduct and frequent desertions, the percentage of native blacks in the unit had dropped to one-third and the enlistments of black Africans had been stopped. The few remaining black troopers were often employed for tracking stock thieves, while their white colleagues performed purely military duties. Between 1817 and 1854, the British always kept a military garrison made up of regulars in South Africa, which usually consisted of four regiments of foot and some companies of the Royal Artillery. No regular cavalry units were sent to the Cape until 1843, when the 7th Dragoon Guards was despatched to South Africa. As happened in Australia, several of the regular foot units serving at the Cape created their own detachments of mounted infantry. The British units and the Cape Mounted Riflemen were supported by the irregular militia of the Boers, which was organized into 'commandos', district-based militia units that could be assembled very rapidly. Their members wore no uniforms, provided their own weapons, elected their own officers in a democratic way and fought as highly mobile mounted infantrymen by employing guerrilla methods. After the Napoleonic Wars, an increasing number of British colonists arrived in South Africa and attempted to organize their own militia, but by 1825 these formations had already disappeared. By 1850, the British regular garrison of the Cape comprised the following infantry units: the 6th Regiment of Foot, 45th Regiment of Foot, 73rd Regiment of Foot and 91st Regiment of Foot. In case of need, these could be supplemented by short-lived volunteer units recruited from the British inhabitants of South Africa or by levies of black irregulars who were loyal to the Crown. In 1850, a major conflict erupted between the British and the Xhosa, and massive reinforcements had to be sent to the Cape: the 2nd Regiment of Foot, 12th Regiment of Foot, 43rd Regiment of Foot, 60th Regiment of Foot, 74th Regiment of Foot, 95th Regiment of Foot and 12th Lancers. The conflict with the Xhosa ended shortly before the outbreak of the Crimean War, which obliged the British authorities to withdraw most of their regular military units from South Africa. In 1856, at the end of the hostilities with Russia, the British tried to expand their garrison at the Cape by sending the recently formed German Legion to South Africa. This unit had a quite peculiar history. At the beginning of the Crimean War, the British Army experienced a serious shortage of manpower, since it was much smaller than its Russian opponent as well as of its French ally. After the end of the Napoleonic Wars, Britain had seriously reduced the size of its military forces to cut costs. The British Army had been restructured mostly to perform garrison duties across the many colonies that it had to protect, and thus Britain was not ready for a full-scale conflict against a major military power on the European continent.

The British authorities were left with no choice but to start recruiting various units of foreign mercenaries in order to sustain their war efforts. Something similar had happened during the Napoleonic Wars, and the British had noticed the positive recent example of the French, who had formed their famous Foreign Legion several years previously. Britain's new foreign units were recruited from areas of Europe where potential soldiers of fortune were available in great numbers: Germany, Switzerland and Italy. These regions were at the time all fragmented into small political entities, making them perfect to provide volunteers for a foreign power such as Britain. In November 1854, the British Parliament passed the Foreign Enlistment Act, according to which foreigners could be enlisted in the British Army for the duration of the conflict with Russia and for service outside the British Isles. During the Napoleonic Wars, the British Army had raised its best foreign units from Germany, in particular from the state of Hanover that was in 'personal union' with Britain (having the same monarch) until the ascent of Queen Victoria to the throne in 1837. When the Crimean War began, the British authorities hastily elaborated plans for the formation of a new German Legion, organized similarly to the effective King's German Legion that had fought in the Napoleonic Wars. The German Prince Albert, consort of Queen Victoria, was enthusiastic about the idea of creating a legion of foreigners from the German princedoms, doing his best to ensure the success of the project. Recruiting operations were organized by the recently appointed commander of the German Legion, Major General Richard von Stutterheim, who hired 200 recruiting agents in Germany and sent them to the major port cities, where large numbers of potential volunteers were available. The recruiters usually went to taverns and bought beer for young adventure-seekers interested in joining the ranks of the legion. By September 1855, despite encountering strong opposition from the governments of the German princedoms, Stutterheim had been able to establish six regiments of light infantry with two battalions each, two regiments of rifles with two battalions each and one regiment of cavalry (light dragoons). These were all sent to training camps in Britain, where they underwent a period of formation. Meanwhile, in Germany, another regiment of rifles was in the process of being formed. Before the Crimean War ended, however, only a handful of units of the German Legion reached the

Contemporary print showing the uniforms worn by the German Legion during the Crimean War; from left to right: rifleman, light infantryman and officer of the light dragoons.

theatre of operations: the 1st Regiment of Light Infantry, the 2nd Regiment of Light Infantry, the 3rd Regiment of Light Infantry and the 1st Regiment of Rifles. None of these saw action, but all of them suffered some losses due to cholera.

Upon disbandment of the legion, the German mercenaries were offered a move to the Cape Colony, where they could settle as military colonists. Each German mercenary received an acre of land in exchange for agreeing to defend the colony from attacks by the local natives. Around 2,300 German soldiers arrived at the Cape in early 1857 and duly became military colonists, being known as the Jager Corps. However, they never adapted to the living conditions in South Africa. In 1858, around 1,400 members of the German Legion – which had not yet formally been disbanded – agreed to leave the Cape and be sent to India in order to fight in the Indian Mutiny. Once again, however, the Germans arrived too late to play any role in the campaign. Around 600 of them returned to South Africa, while the others joined the ranks of the East India Company's European military units. What remained of the German Legion was officially disbanded in 1861, several of its surviving members having joined the ranks of the Cape Mounted Riflemen. From 1852, several troops of white mounted police had been raised on the frontier of South Africa to act as a paramilitary constabulary, and in 1855 these were assembled together and embodied as the Frontier Armed and Mounted Police. This unit comprised 500 men, who were responsible for their own horses, weapons and rations. In 1855, to revive the system of the commandos that was disappearing due to the migration of the Boers, a Burgher Act introduced compulsory commando service. However, the new law proved ineffective as the obligation it prescribed was limited to the burgher's home district. Since 1852, several volunteer military corps had been raised from the British inhabitants of South Africa, which were mostly formed in or around Cape Town. Several of these were quite short-lived, while others earned a solid reputation, such as the Cape Rifle Corps, formed in 1855 with two companies, and the Port Elizabeth Volunteer Rifle Corps, created in 1856 and consisting of a single company.

The Great Trek led to the formation of several new autonomous Boer states on the north-eastern border of South Africa, which struggled against the local native communities to expand their territories. The Boers were jealous of their independence, and their newly formed political entities were thus republics that did not recognize the suzerainty of the British Crown. In 1839, after obtaining a significant victory over the Zulu at the Battle of Blood River, they established the Natalia Republic on the territory of present-day Natal. Initially, the British authorities did very little to exert control over the new Boer state, but when the Boers made contact with some Dutch representatives they decided to act in order to prevent the transformation of Natal into a colony of the Netherlands. A British expeditionary force occupied the

Natalia Republic during 1842, having defeated the local Boer forces. Two years later, Natal was annexed to the Cape Colony and remained part of it until being organized as an autonomous colony in 1854. Most of the Boers who had created the Natalia Republic, not wishing to become British subjects, trekked over the mountains that marked the new north-eastern border of the Cape Colony. In a period of some ten years, they settled over a vast territory extending north of the Orange River. In 1852, the British government signed the Sand River Convention with the 40,000 Boer people living north-east of the Cape Colony. Under the convention, the lands located between the Orange River in the south and the Vaal River in the north were organized as an autonomous Boer state placed under British suzerainty, while the Boer lands north of the Vaal River were completely independent from British rule. The southern Boer state became known as the Orange Free State in 1854, while the northern one assumed the denomination of the Transvaal Republic. By signing the Sand River Convention, the British hoped to create a buffer zone in the form of the Orange Free State between their colonial possessions and the independent Boer lands. The Boers, however, continued expanding their territories, which was bound to cause major conflicts with the Zulu, something that the British wanted to avoid. The Orange Free State was often hostile to the indirect British rule, and thus supported the Transvaal Republic, throwing the British plans into disarray. Since 1848, Natal had, in addition to a British garrison of regular troops, a locally raised constabulary force of 150 men known as the Natal Native Police, but this was disbanded in 1854. During the same year, the first volunteer military corps were formed in Natal: the Durban Volunteer Guard, Royal Durban Rangers and Natal Carabineers. The first of these was gradually expanded and came to comprise an artillery company, which in 1870 became an independent corps with the denomination of the Durban Volunteer Artillery. Differently from the Durban Volunteer Guard, both the Royal Durban Rangers and the Natal Carabineers were small mounted units. From 1866, the latter were supplemented by the Natal Native Horse, a new cavalry corps raised from Bantu natives who were loyal to the Crown (many of whom had converted to Christianity). Both the Orange Free State and the Transvaal Republic had their own military forces, which consisted of irregular Boer commandos.

In 1872, the Cape Colony was granted internal self-government by Britain and the British garrison in South Africa was significantly reduced. As a result, new military and paramilitary units had to be raised on a local basis in order to secure the defence of the colony's frontiers. In 1870, the Cape Mounted Riflemen had been disbanded due to the lack of suitable native recruits. The existing Frontier Armed and Mounted Police was renamed the Cape Mounted Riflemen in 1878. Four years before, the unit had formed its own artillery detachment, which was equipped with mountain

Officer of the Cape Mounted Riflemen in the 1860s. (*ASKB Military Collection*)

guns. The 1870s saw the proliferation of new paramilitary police units in South Africa. In 1873, the Northern Border Police was created, which was amalgamated with the Frontier Armed and Mounted Police in 1877 before being disbanded in 1881. The small Griqualand Police was formed in 1877 and dissolved in 1881, while the Basutoland Mounted Police was raised in 1872 from friendly individuals of the Basuto natives. In addition to these there were the volunteer corps, most of which were active in Cape Town. These included the Cape Rifle Corps (which assumed the name of the Duke of Edinburgh's Own Volunteer Rifles in 1860), the Port

Elizabeth Volunteer Rifle Corps (later re-named Prince Alfred's Guard), the Cape Town Cavalry (a cavalry troop formed in 1857, whose members were nicknamed The Sparklers), the Cape Town Volunteer Artillery (an artillery company formed in 1857, members of which could handle both coastal and field guns) and the Port Elizabeth Volunteer Artillery (raised in 1860). The diamond-producing area located around Kimberley known as Griqualand – which remained autonomous until 1881 – had since 1876 a volunteer mounted corps called the Diamond Fields Horse. In 1878, the new military units of South Africa were tested during a frontier war against the Bantu. This proved disastrous for the corps fielded by the Cape Colony, to the point

Officer (left) and trooper (right) of the Cape Mounted Riflemen in the 1870s. The officer is wearing a patrol jacket, a military garment that was very popular for campaign use in South Africa. (*ASKB Military Collection*)

that the British government had to intervene by sending massive reinforcements. The mix of Frontier Armed and Mounted Police, volunteer corps, Burgher Force (irregular Boer commandos) and native levies showed all their limits in terms of cohesion and discipline. Consequently, after the end of hostilities, the military forces of South Africa had to be completely reorganized. The Frontier Armed and Mounted Police, as we have seen, was fully militarized and given the new name of the Cape Mounted Riflemen. Three Cape Mounted Yeomanry Regiments were raised in the eastern areas of South Africa to support them, each of which acted as a highly mobile striking force with ten troops of sixty men. Several new volunteer units, all having the numerical consistency of a cavalry troop, were raised, while the services provided by the Boers in the form of commandos was regulated through the Burgher Forces and Levies Act. This introduced payment for those Boers who wished to serve under the British flag. In Natal, the new Natal Mounted Police, mustering 150 men, was formed in 1874 to supplement the few locally raised volunteer corps, most of which were stationed in Durban.

In January 1879, the Anglo-Zulu War broke out, following years of growing tensions between the Transvaal Republic and the Zulu Kingdom. The exact frontier between Boer and Zulu lands had never been clearly defined, which represented a serious problem for the Boers, especially after the Zulu started to be ruled by a warlike king – Cetshwayo – who carried out an expansionist policy and transformed the Zulu fighting forces into the most formidable native army of its time in Africa. Keen to strengthen their political control over the Transvaal Republic – which had been formally annexed to the British colonial possessions in 1877 – and limit the military power of the Zulu, the British authorities invaded Zululand. The Anglo-Zulu War mostly affected the territory of Natal, which was required to form several military corps to act as auxiliaries for the main invasion force, which consisted almost entirely of British regular infantry. The first invasion of Zululand carried out by the British ended in complete failure, suffering an overwhelming defeat at the Battle of Isandlwana on 22 January 1879. Following the arrival of massive reinforcements from Britain, a second and this time successful invasion was launched, culminating in a decisive British victory at the Battle of Ulundi on 4 July 1879. The following auxiliary corps, mostly raised in Natal, participated in the British conquest of Zululand, in addition to the Natal Mounted Police:

Natal Native Contingent: being levied from the natives of Natal who were loyal to the Crown, this consisted of seven infantry battalions assembled into three regiments. Each battalion had ten companies and each company comprised a cadre of white officers and NCOs. After the first invasion, it was reorganized on five battalions.

Natal Native Mounted Contingent: being levied from the natives living in the foothills of Natal, it consisted of six cavalry troops. After the first invasion, it was reorganized on six independent and smaller new troops.

Natal Native Pioneers: raised by tribal leaders who were loyal to the Crown, it consisted of three companies of native pioneers who were commanded by white officers.

Border Guard: before the invasion of Zululand, the territory of Natal was divided into seven Defensive Districts, three of which were known as Border Districts as they bordered the territory of the Zulu. These three districts raised a Border Guard of 300–350 native men, as a well as a Border Guard Reserve that was to be called to serve only in case of enemy invasion.

Dunn's Foot Scouts: this was a force of 150 Zulu auxiliaries raised by John Dunn, a trader and hunter who had earned a chiefdom in Zululand thanks to the military services provided to Cetshwayo. After the outbreak of the Anglo-Zulu War, Dunn sided with the British authorities.

Wood's Irregulars: this was a force of 2,000 Swazi auxiliaries raised by Colonel Evelyn Wood and assembled into two battalions.

Natal Carabineers: a volunteer corps formed as early as 1855 and comprising a single cavalry troop.

Buffalo Border Guard: a volunteer corps existing since 1873 and consisting of a single cavalry troop.

Newcastle Mounted Rifles: a volunteer cavalry troop formed in 1875.

Victoria Mounted Rifles: a volunteer corps formed as early as 1862 and having a single cavalry troop.

Stanger Mounted Rifles: a volunteer cavalry troop formed in 1875.

Durban Mounted Rifles: a volunteer cavalry troop formed in 1873.

Natal Hussars: a volunteer corps formed as early as 1865 and consisting of a single cavalry troop.

Alexandra Mounted Rifles: a volunteer corps formed as early as 1865 and comprising a single cavalry troop.

Isipingo Mounted Rifles: a volunteer cavalry troop raised in 1878.

Frontier Light Horse: four troops of irregular cavalrymen, the first three of which were created in 1877.

Natal Light Horse: formed in 1879, it was an irregular corps of cavalry mustering 138 men.

Baker's Horse: formed in 1878, it was an irregular corps of cavalry with 224 men.

Lonsdale's Horse: four troops of irregular cavalry, raised for the Anglo-Zulu War.

Natal Horse: three troops of irregular cavalry, formed for the second invasion of Zululand.

Carbutt's Border Rangers: a small irregular corps of cavalry, mustering twenty-one whites and twenty-two natives.

Kaffrarian Riflemen: raised by a veteran of the German Legion, it consisted of 113 irregular cavalrymen.

Raaff's Transvaal Rangers: a corps of irregular cavalry raised in 1878 and mustering 150 men (100 Boers and fifty individuals of mixed descent).

Weatherley's Border Horse: two troops of irregular cavalry formed in 1878.

Transvaal Burgher Force: fifty Boers from Transvaal who acted as scouts and skirmishers thanks to their excellent knowledge of the local terrain.

In addition to the above units, there were also two corps of volunteer infantry – the Royal Durban Rifles and Maritzburg Rifles – that did not participate in the military operations. Transvaal, which had been annexed by the British shortly before the invasion of Zululand, contributed to the war effort by providing just a couple of volunteer corps that were raised from the few British settlers living on its territory. The Boers refused to enlist in significant numbers to support the British

Army, forming just one noticeable corps – known as Ferreira's Horse – that provided some excellent irregular mounted riflemen. In 1880, the Boers of Transvaal had risen up in revolt against the British Empire, in what became known as the First Boer War, which ended up with a British defeat at the Battle of Majuba in 1881 and the restoration of Transvaal's republican independence. Following the conquest of Zululand, which saw the participation of just a few military units from the Cape Colony, the fighting forces of South Africa entered a period of reorganization and consolidation. The artillery troop of the Cape Mounted Riflemen was detached from its parent unit and became autonomous as the Cape Field Artillery. In 1881, the three Yeomanry Regiments were disbanded; a year later, a new paramilitary constabulary corps, the Cape Police Force, was formed. An experimental regular battalion, known as the Cape Infantry and raised from British reservists who lived in South Africa, was created in 1882. This, however, was disbanded for economic reasons in 1886. During 1884, compulsory registration of Boer men for the Burgher Force was ended, effectively disbanding what remained of the Boer militia based on commandos. Two new volunteer corps – the Cape Town Highlanders and Cape Town Irish Volunteer Rifles – were created in 1885 from the Scottish and Irish communities at Cape Town. During 1891, the new Cape Garrison Artillery was raised to support the

Troopers of the Natal Carabineers (left), Durban Mounted Rifles (centre) and Frontier Light Horse (right) in 1879. (*Colour plate by Patricio Greve Moller, copyright of Gabriele Esposito*)

Cape Field Artillery, converting an existing corps of volunteers known as the Cape Town Volunteer Engineers. In 1896, the Cape Field Artillery and Cape Garrison Artillery were combined to form the new Cape Artillery. Meanwhile, in Zululand, a new police corps, the Zululand Native Police, had been formed in 1883 to garrison the newly conquered territories alongside the British regulars. In 1892, the Natal Field Artillery was formed in Natal.

In October 1899, the Second Boer War broke out between Britain and the Boer states (Transvaal Republic and Orange Free State). Following the discovery of large deposits of gold on the land inhabited by the Boers, thousands of British settlers from Cape Town moved to the Boer states, where they were not welcomed by the local communities. The British, seeking control over the large amounts of gold that had just been found, opened hostilities with the Boers. The new conflict lasted until 1902 and began with a series of striking victories for the Boers. The British responded by sending massive reinforcements to South Africa and invading the two Boer states with an army of 180,000 men. In 1900, both the Transvaal Republic and Orange Free State were annexed to the British Empire, but the Boers mounted strong resistance. They attacked the British invaders using hit-and-run guerrilla tactics and frequent ambushes. For two years, the British regulars had to deal with the commandos, suffering heavy losses until the employment of very harsh repressive methods – which included the building of concentration camps and the use of scorched earth politics – finally obtained victory for the British counter-insurgence. In 1910, eight years after the end of the war, Transvaal and the Orange Free State were united with the Cape Colony and Natal to form the new Union of South Africa, a self-governing dominion of the British Empire. The Second Boer War was mostly fought by British regulars and newly raised volunteer corps that were formed in Britain, as well as by contingents provided by some of Britain's largest colonies, such as Canada and Australia. India provided a single cavalry squadron – Lumsden's Force – that was recruited from white settlers, while Ceylon sent two companies of mounted infantry recruited from white planters. When the hostilities began, South Africa forces consisted of three main units: the Cape Mounted Riflemen with 940 men, the Cape Police with 700 men and the Cape Artillery. Quite soon, however, the British regular troops operating against the Boers started to suffer from a lack of mounted units, so several new cavalry corps had to be raised from the local communities of the Cape Colony. These included the Imperial Light Horse and South African Light Horse (the latter having three regiments), as well as a smaller unit called the Commander in Chief's Bodyguard. These were later merged together as a Colonial Division tasked with a series of auxiliary duties. In 1901, the new Colonial Defence Force was formed to protect South Africa from incursions by the Boer commandos. It comprised of dozens of Town Guards and District Mounted Troops, which were raised for local defence and had a part-time nature. In December 1901, the Colonial Division and Colonial Defence Force merged to create the new Cape Colonial Forces. Natal, following the example of the Cape Colony, formed its own Volunteer Brigade,

Zulu warriors from the 1870s. The native levies recruited by the British in South Africa consisted of warriors clothed according to their traditional fashions. (*ASKB Military Collection*)

Trooper of the Cape Police Force in 1885.

mostly comprising light horse units. Meanwhile, in 1900, the British created a new paramilitary corps on the Boer territories, the South African Constabulary, which played a prominent role in the counter-guerrilla operations that were conducted until 1902. A small number of Boers decided to side with Britain during the Second Boer

War. Those from Transvaal were assembled into the National Scouts (1,000 men), while those from the Orange Free State formed the Orange River Colony Volunteers (500 men).

After 1902, the armed forces of South Africa were completely reorganized, with all the units raised during the previous years disbanded. A Royal Garrison Regiment was formed from British recalled reservists who had volunteered to remain in South Africa after the end of the war. This garrisoned the former Boer territories until being disbanded in 1908. From 1904, Natal started to form its own militia, which replaced most of the existing volunteer corps. The two former Boer states continued to be garrisoned by the South African Constabulary (mustering five mobile troops, each having some light artillery pieces) until it was divided into two autonomous police corps in 1908: the Transvaal Police and Orange River Colony Police. In 1910, following the creation of the Union of South Africa, a new military structure was formed in order to assemble the military resources of four different colonies (Cape Colony, Natal, Transvaal and Orange River Colony). In 1912, a Defence Act was passed, which prescribed the creation of a unified Union Defence Force, which comprised a small Permanent Force made up of regulars and a part-time Active Citizen Force of volunteers. The Defence Act debarred non-whites from military service. The Permanent Force consisted of five regiments of South African Mounted Rifles, each of which had an artillery detachment. These were raised from former members of the best military units that existed before 1910, such as the Cape Mounted Riflemen. A separate South African Police was made responsible for keeping law and order in the white settlements, while the Permanent Force patrolled areas inhabited by native communities. The Active Citizen Force consisted of four kinds of troops: Mounted Rifles (obtained from former volunteer corps), Dismounted Rifles (newly raised units that had to be mobilized and given horses only in case of need), Infantry and Artillery. There were nineteen regiments of Mounted Rifles, fourteen regiments of Dismounted Rifles, twelve regiments of Infantry and eight batteries of Artillery (three equipped with field pieces and five with horse-drawn pieces). In addition, there was a part-time volunteer Coast Garrison Force tasked with manning the coastal defences at Cape Town and Durban. In case of war mobilization, South Africa could provide the British Empire with three infantry brigades – with four battalions and one artillery detachment each – plus five regiments of mounted rifles.

Chapter 6

India

The British presence in India became significant from the mid-eighteenth century, particularly after the Battle of Plassey in 1757. Until then, other European colonial powers like France and Portugal had exerted a greater influence over India than did Britain. Since the times of the first territorial acquisitions in the Indian subcontinent, the British government had not annexed any Indian territory as a direct possession of the Crown; from a formal and practical point of view, the British territories in India were all under the control of the East India Company (EIC). Established in 1600, the EIC was a joint-stock company whose original main objective was to trade with the rich countries of the Asian continent. Like its Dutch equivalent operating in present-day Indonesia, the British East India Company gradually emerged as a regional power in Asia, expanding its commercial influence by political and military means. The British traders gradually started to occupy important cities in India and several tracts of coastline. All these new territories acted as outposts for the economic activities of the EIC and were also centres from which the British could exert their political influence over the local Indian rulers. By the middle of the eighteenth century, with the decline of the great Moghul Empire, India was fractioned into a multitude of independent princedoms. These had outdated armies using traditional Indian weaponry and tactics, which were no match for the modern military technologies employed by the British. As a result of this, the EIC could gradually use its great economic resources to transform several native Indian states into protectorates. Thanks to the signing of favourable treaties concerning trade, the British acquired direct control over an increasing number of cities and territories. After their great victory at Plassey, with which the French were expelled from most of India, the British could expand their possessions towards the interior of the subcontinent. Consequently, during the following decades, the East India Company was obliged to reorganize its military forces: initially very small, their main task was to protect the commercial interests of the Company and garrisoning its territorial possessions. From their foundation, the military forces of the EIC included a number of native soldiers. These were recruited with the help of local rulers who were allies of the Company and made up a private military organization that was not part of the British Army. On many occasions, the European and native components

Private of the Bengal European Infantry in 1815. (*Colour plate by Patricio Greve Moller, copyright of Gabriele Esposito*)

NCO of the Bengal Native Infantry in 1815. The blue headgear was peculiar to the Bengal foot troops.

Private of the Bengal Native Infantry in 1825. (*ASKB Military Collection*)

NCO of the Bengal Native Infantry in 1845. (*ASKB Military Collection*)

Private (left) and NCO (right) of the Bengal Native Infantry in 1850.

British officer from a rifle company of the Bengal Native Infantry in the 1840s. (*ASKB Military Collection*)

India 111

Privates from a rifle company (left) and a fusilier company (right) of the Bengal Native Infantry in 1855. The headgear is protected by a white cover. (*ASKB Military Collection*)

of the EIC's forces cooperated well and proved very efficient on the battlefield.

With the reorganization that followed Plassey, they also started to have significant numbers and their standards of service became comparable to those of contemporary European armies. The military units at the service of the EIC could be European in nature, made up of soldiers coming from Europe, or native corps recruited from the local population but having British officers. The Indian soldiers serving European powers, be they Hindus or Muslims, were commonly known as sepoys. Generally speaking, the European soldiers recruited by the Company in Britain were not of the same quality as those who served in the regular British Army. Indeed, the British Army offered better conditions of service to recruits, meaning the best elements wishing to serve in the military usually entered the ranks of the regulars. Most of the British soldiers serving under the flags of the EIC were individuals who had decided to leave their country in search of money or adventure and lived at the margins of their home society. Some of them had experienced problems with justice while others had no choice but to enlist as soldiers of fortune in order to earn a living. Members of the European military units also comprised significant numbers of whites who were recruited in India from all the European adventurers or mercenaries

Trooper from the Governor General's Bodyguard of Bengal in 1815.

India 113

NCO of the Bengal Native Cavalry in 1820. (*ASKB Military Collection*)

British officer of the Bengal Native Cavalry in the 1840s, wearing parade dress. (*ASKB Military Collection*)

there who were in search of employment. French, Swiss, German and Dutch recruits were the most common, but there were also individuals of mixed ancestry (half-European and half-Indian). The discipline and training of these soldiers were not as high as their equivalents serving in the British Army, but on most occasions they proved to be reliable fighters. A good number of them had a clear idea of what military discipline was, since it was not uncommon for a soldier from the British Army to choose to become part of the Company's forces after his period of service had ended. Life in India was cheaper than in Britain and the risks faced while serving under the flags of the Company were not comparable to those experienced with the British Army.

At the beginning of the nineteenth century, the territorial possessions of the British East India Company were organized into three autonomous presidencies: Bengal, Madras and Bombay. Each of these had its own army. During the first half of the eighteenth century, each of the armies of the EIC's presidencies recruited auxiliary infantry companies of Indian native soldiers when needed, notably in case of war. These corps had a temporary and semi-regular nature. The combat experience gained during the Seven Years' War, and particularly at the Battle of Plassey, however, showed the EIC the great potential of the locally recruited contingents, so from 1757, the existing independent and temporary companies of sepoys were consolidated into permanent, well-disciplined battalions with European officers. In the Bengal Army, most of the sepoys were Hindus of high caste, who came in great numbers from the Indian provinces bordering Bengal. In Madras and Bombay, however, as well as high-caste Hindus there were large numbers of Muslims. Generally speaking, all the native soldiers serving the East India Company came from the martial races of India, social groups characterized by specific ethnic and cultural features which were traditionally linked with the profession of soldiery in India. At the beginning of the Seven Years' War in 1756, the European infantry of Bengal consisted of a single company with 150 men, most of whom were Dutch or Eurasians; the artillery consisted of a single company. After the victory at Plassey, however, the European infantry of Bengal was increased to a full regiment that assumed the denomination of the Bengal European Regiment, while the artillery was expanded to two companies (later increased to four). In 1765, by retaining in service many European soldiers of fortune who had fought in India during the Seven Years' War, it was possible to expand the European infantry of the Bengal Presidency to three regiments. Under the orders of Robert Clive, the victor of Plassey, Bengal was the first presidency to assemble its sepoy companies into a battalion. These fought with great distinction at Plassey, which encouraged the EIC to form more locally raised infantry units drilled and equipped in European fashion. By 1762, the number of native infantry battalions in Bengal

British officer of the Bengal Native Cavalry in the 1840s, wearing service dress. (*ASKB Military Collection*)

Trooper of the Bengal Native Cavalry in the 1840s. (*ASKB Military Collection*)

Trooper of the irregular Skinner's Horse in the 1830s. (*ASKB Military Collection*)

had risen to twenty-one, but this figure was reduced to eighteen in 1763 after three of the units were disbanded following a mutiny. By 1775, there were twenty-one battalions of sepoys again, organized as follows: the 1st–7th Battalions formed a 1st Brigade, those numbered 8–14 formed a 2nd Brigade and those numbered 15–21 a 3rd Brigade. By 1781, the native infantry of Bengal had been expanded to forty-two battalions, but with the demobilization that followed the end of the American Revolution these were reorganized into twenty-nine regiments, each having two battalions.

Initially, the EIC did not raise any cavalry unit for service in its Indian colonial possessions, as maintaining mounted formations had enormous economic costs. However, it soon became apparent that large numbers of Indian auxiliaries were available for establishing some small but efficient cavalry corps. Bengal's early native cavalry consisted of just three troops of local horsemen, known as the Moghul Horse because their members were equipped as heavy cavalrymen in traditional Moghul style, with metal helmets and cuirasses. These three troops of native cavalry were assembled together in 1772 in order to form a single unit that was renamed the Governor General's Bodyguard in 1781. Between 1776 and 1778, another two regiments of native cavalry were formed by regularizing the auxiliary mounted contingents provided by various Indian princedoms. By 1797, the Bengal Army comprised three regiments of European infantry with one battalion each, twelve regiments of native infantry with two battalions each, four regiments of native cavalry and three battalions of artillery. The artillery units in all three presidencies

Trooper of the irregular Rohilla Cavalry in the 1830s. (*Colour plate by Patricio Greve Moller, copyright of Gabriele Esposito*)

Gunner of the Bengal Native Artillery in 1825. (*ASKB Military Collection*)

Officers of the Bengal European Artillery in the late 1840s. Some of the figures are wearing undress uniform with peaked cap. (*ASKB Military Collection*)

were entirely made up of Europeans, who underwent the same training as their colleagues from the Royal Artillery and thus were soldiers of excellent quality. In 1803, James Skinner brought a regiment of irregular cavalry raised in Scinde into the EIC's service, the unit later becoming known as Skinner's Horse. During 1804 and 1805, the armed forces of the Bengal Presidency underwent a radical reorganization, at the end of which they mustered one regiment of European infantry (the Bengal European Regiment), twenty-four battalions of native infantry, nine regiments of native cavalry (including the Governor General's Bodyguard), three battalions of

Trooper of the Bengal Horse Artillery in 1846. (*ASKB Military Collection*)

Native officer of the Bengal Horse Artillery in 1848. (*ASKB Military Collection*)

European foot artillery, one company of native sappers and one company of native pioneers. The first troop of horse artillery, always made up of white soldiers, was raised in 1806. There were seven troops of horse artillery in Bengal by 1818, one of which was equipped with rockets. In 1818, three new troops of native horse artillerymen were added in order to form a consolidated regiment. The following year, the units of Bengal native cavalry were collectively renamed as the Bengal Light Horse. During that same year, the sappers and pioneers were merged into a single Corps of

Officer (left) and private (right) of the Madras Native Infantry in the 1830s.

Officer of the Madras European Infantry in 1845.

Sappers and Miners. Like the other two presidencies, Bengal had a small Engineer Corps consisting of a few British officers with specific technical skills. These were at the head of the locally raised labour force of sappers and pioneers recruited from Indians. The success of Skinner's Horse led to the creation of more contingents of irregular cavalry that were recruited with the *sillidar* system, according to which – in return for a higher rate of pay – each irregular recruit provided his own horse and equipment in addition to his rations. Only firearms and ammunition were paid for by the EIC. By 1823, the Bengal Army comprised five regiments of irregular cavalry: Skinner's Horse, Gardner's Horse, the Rohilla Cavalry, Baddeley's Frontier Horse and Gough's Horse.

Between 1814 and 1816, the East India Company was at war with the Kingdom of Nepal, a warlike nation located on the north-eastern border of India, south of the Himalayas. The exact frontier dividing the territory of Nepal from the portion of India controlled by the British had never been clearly defined, which led to escalating tensions during the early years of the nineteenth century between the EIC and Nepal. An important regional power of northern India for some time, Nepal considered British colonial expansion a great threat. The territory of Nepal has long been inhabited by many

Private of the Madras European Infantry in 1845. (*ASKB Military Collection*)

Uniforms of the Madras Native Infantry in the 1840s.

different tribal groups, most of which are of Mongolian descent. By the beginning of the nineteenth century, the Gurkhas had risen to prominence and controlled the political life of the Nepalese realm. The mountain terrain of Nepal has affected the physical characteristics of the people living on it, giving them the sturdy build and muscular legs developed by all mountain peoples. Nepalese warriors have always been excellent light infantrymen, used to travelling long distances on foot and to fighting on harsh mountain terrain. Being highly mobile and capable of surviving with very modest rations, during the Anglo-Nepalese War of 1814–1816 they defeated EIC forces on several occasions. Thanks to their capabilities as mountain infantry, the Gurkha warriors employed guerrilla tactics with great success, setting ambushes and causing significant losses to the enemy without being intercepted. Armed with flintlock muskets and deadly knives with a curved blade – the *kukri* – they were admired by their British enemies for their incredible courage. In 1816, due to the decisive numerical superiority of the EIC's troops, Nepal was forced to end hostilities by signing a peace treaty that gave the British much of the contested frontier areas. After 1816, however, the Kingdom of Nepal became Britain's most loyal and trusted ally in India. In 1815,

British officer from a rifle company of the Madras Native Infantry in 1845.

Private from a rifle company of the Madras Native Infantry in the late 1830s.

British officer of the Madras Native Cavalry in the early 1840s, wearing parade dress.

British officer of the Madras Native Cavalry in the late 1830s, wearing undress uniform.

many Gurkha warriors captured by the British had agreed to enter the ranks of the EIC forces. As a result, the first four battalions of Gurkha light infantry were formed in the Bengal Army: the 1st Nasiri Battalion, 2nd Nasiri Battalion, Sirmoor Battalion and Kumaon Provincial Battalion. In 1824, a further Gurkha unit – the Sylhet Local Battalion – was formed, and in 1826 the two Nasiri Battalions were consolidated as a single unit.

Native officer of the Madras Native Cavalry in the late 1830s.

During 1824 and 1825, the Bengal Army underwent a significant reorganization. The native infantry was restructured on seventy-four regiments, each having one battalion, which included the four elite Gurkha units. Each of the native infantry battalions had eight companies of fusiliers, one company of grenadiers and one of light infantry. In 1840, three new regiments of light infantry were created by assembling together the light infantry companies of various battalions that were already in existence. As for the European infantry, it was progressively enlarged with

British officer of the Madras Native Cavalry in the early 1850s. (*ASKB Military Collection*)

the formation of two new regiments: the 2nd Bengal European Regiment in 1839 (later renamed the Bengal Fusiliers) and the Bengal European Light Infantry in 1859. The single unit existing before 1839 assumed the denomination of the Royal Bengal Fusiliers. During the 1840s, the EIC fought two major wars (the first in 1845–1846 and the second in 1848–1849) against the powerful Sikh Empire in present-day north-western India and Pakistan. Since 1799, the Sikh state had been

Officer of the Madras European Artillery in the late 1830s, wearing undress uniform.

Native officer of the Madras Native Artillery in the late 1830s.

Gunner of the Madras Native Artillery in the late 1830s.

NCO (left) and officer (right) of the Madras Horse Artillery in 1845. (*ASKB Military Collection*)

one of the most important regional military powers of northern India. It controlled the large region of Punjab and was dominated by a caste of professional warriors, who adhered to a peculiar monotheistic religion that was characterized by a series of specific practices. The term 'Sikhs' means 'lions' in the language spoken in Punjab, confirming the great importance that was attributed to personal combat skills by all members of the Sikh warrior caste. The British suffered several defeats during the two wars fought against the Sikh Empire and were engaged in numerous pitched battles before they were able to annex Punjab in 1849. Like happened with the Gurkhas of Nepal, the Sikhs of Punjab started to be recruited into the army of the EIC after having been defeated. Already in 1846, having been impressed by the great combat

British NCO of the Madras Horse Artillery in 1845, wearing campaign dress. (*ASKB Military Collection*)

abilities of the Sikhs, the EIC had raised two infantry regiments from Punjab. These were soon supplemented by a Frontier Brigade, which mustered four Sikh infantry regiments as well as an elite Corps of Guides consisting of two companies of infantry and one troop of cavalry (later increased – respectively – to six and three). The Corps of Guides was tasked with garrisoning the north-western frontier of British India and comprised battle-hardened veterans. In 1849, the Frontier Brigade became part of a larger Transfrontier Brigade that comprised five infantry regiments (later

Native officer of the Madras Horse Artillery in the late 1830s.

Officer of the Bombay European Infantry in 1845, wearing undress uniform with peaked cap.

Native officer of the Bombay Native Infantry in 1845, wearing parade dress with shako. (*ASKB Military Collection*)

Uniforms of the Bombay Native Infantry in the late 1840s; from left to right: NCO, British officer and private.

increased to six) and five regiments of irregular cavalry, in addition to the Corps of Guides. The Transfrontier Brigade later became known as the Punjab Frontier Force or Punjab Irregular Force.

As for mounted troops, until 1825 the Bengal Light Cavalry consisted of eight regiments in addition to the Governor General's Bodyguard. Two new regiments were formed by 1826, bringing the total to ten. These were supplemented by the various irregular corps recruited according to the *sillidar* system, which were called the Bengal Local Horse until their name was changed to the Bengal Irregular

Private from the Belooch Native Infantry in 1848. The infantry units raised from Balochistan were always dressed in emerald green with red facings, which made them very easy to recognize on the battlefield. (*Colour plate by Patricio Greve Moller, copyright of Gabriele Esposito*)

British officer of the Bombay Native Cavalry in 1846. (*ASKB Military Collection*)

British officer of the irregular Scinde Horse in the early 1850s.

Cavalry in 1840. The irregular mounted troops were reduced to five units in 1829, but during the following years they were progressively expanded; by 1846, they consisted of eighteen units. The five regiments of irregular cavalry that were part of the Punjab Frontier Force were completely autonomous from the Bengal Irregular Cavalry, being collectively known as Punjab Cavalry. Since 1815, the Bengal Army had comprised several units of irregular infantry (collectively known as Bengal Local

Infantry), which were recruited under the same system used for the corps of irregular cavalry; these mostly performed auxiliary duties, and by 1823 there were sixteen units. Another fourteen such corps, which had a variable numerical consistency, were formed between 1830 and 1856. Several contingents of irregular auxiliaries were also provided by the Indian princedoms that were allied with the EIC. The six Sikh infantry regiments of the Punjab Frontier Force were completely independent from the Bengal Local Infantry. Between 1825 and 1856, the artillery of the Bengal Army was significantly expanded and came to comprise an increasing number of native soldiers. By 1856, it mustered three brigades of horse artillery (each with three European troops and one native troop), five battalions of European foot artillery (each with five companies) and two battalions of native foot artillery (each with two companies). The Corps of Sappers and Miners had expanded to six companies by 1856.

Around 1720, Madras had three European infantry companies, which included a substantial number of Eurasians. There was also a small artillery corps, comprising a number of native 'lascars' (workers). In 1748, the armed forces of the Madras Presidency were expanded with the addition of two new infantry companies recruited from Swiss professional soldiers, being reorganized as a single battalion of infantry supported by one company of artillery. In 1758, the infantry was expanded with the addition of another two battalions. In 1774, the three existing European foot units were restructured as two infantry regiments with two battalions each. The artillery was expanded to two companies in 1752 and then three in 1765. The native infantry of Madras was grouped into two permanent battalions during 1759, each comprising eight companies of fusiliers and one of grenadiers. In 1759, the number of native battalions in Madras was increased to six, the expansion continuing after the end of the Seven Years' War so that by 1767 there were nineteen battalions of native infantry in the presidency. In 1748, the first troop of cavalry was raised in Madras; this, consisting of Europeans, was disbanded in 1752 but was re-formed in 1758. In 1761, the number of cavalry troops was increased to four, each consisting of five officers and sixty other ranks. In 1772, the European cavalry of Madras was disbanded. From 1767, the presidency could also count on 8 native cavalry regiments with 500 men each, provided by the Nawab of Arcot (an ally of the East India Company). Following a mutiny, these were later reduced to four regiments. In 1770, the native infantry of the Madras Army was reorganized on eighteen battalions, split into two separate groups: thirteen were known as Carnatic Battalions and were based in the southern areas of the presidency, while the remaining five Circar Battalions were based in the northern part of the presidency. A new unit of native cavalry, known as the Governor's Bodyguard, was raised in 1778. In 1784, the distinction

Trooper of the irregular Scinde Horse in the early 1850s. (*ASKB Military Collection*)

British officer of the Bombay Horse Artillery in 1846. (*ASKB Military Collection*)

between Carnatic and Circar Battalions was abolished, and four new regiments of native cavalry were raised to replace those provided by the Nawab of Arcot that were dissolved due to indiscipline. By 1796, the Madras Army consisted of two regiments of European infantry, eleven regiments of native infantry (with two battalions each), four regiments of native cavalry and two battalions of artillery (each of the latter having five companies of white artillerymen and fifteen companies of Indian lascars).

Between 1796 and 1824, the native infantry of Madras saw a progressive but significant expansion, with the number of regiments – always having two battalions each – increased to twenty-five. From 1810, the Madras Army included an elite Madras Rifle Corps, which consisted of eight companies and was formed from the best marksmen of the various native infantry battalions. In 1811, four of these companies were defined as 'light' units. During 1830, the Madras Rifle Corps was disbanded. By 1824, the native cavalry consisted of the Governor's Bodyguard – which from 1808 was formed only on special occasions by assembling the best

Private of the Gurkha infantry in 1816. The Gurkha units were dressed in dark green, the distinctive colour of the British Army's rifle units, from their creation. Note the presence of the deadly *kukri*, the knife of the Gurkhas. (*ASKB Military Collection*)

Private of the Gurkha infantry in the early 1840s. The headgear has a white protective cover. (*ASKB Military Collection*)

elements from the various native mounted units – plus eight regiments. The first horse artillery unit of Madras was created in 1805 and consisted of a single European troop. By 1819, this had been expanded to comprise two European troops, three native troops and a special troop equipped with rockets. In 1818, a single company of sappers and miners was formed in Madras to act as the labour force of

Infantry officer (with round shield) and privates from the Sikh Frontier Brigade in 1848. The Sikh Corps of Guides, raised in 1846, was the first military unit in the world to adopt khaki as the main colour of its dress. (*ASKB Military Collection*)

the local Engineer Corps. However, the unit was quite short-lived, being disbanded in 1821. In 1824, the native infantry of the Madras Army was restructured on fifty single-battalion regiments, and by 1830 the number of battalion-sized regiments had been increased to fifty-two. The native cavalry continued to comprise eight regiments until 1857, supported by the mounted units of the Hyderabad Contingent. The latter was provided to the Madras Presidency by the Nizam of Hyderabad, one of the most powerful Indian monarchs and a loyal ally of the EIC. The semi-regular

Cavalry troopers (left) and officer (right) of the Punjab Frontier Force in the early 1850s. (*ASKB Military Collection*)

Hyderabad Contingent, established in 1826, had British officers and comprised five cavalry regiments as well as eight infantry regiments. The European infantry consisted of a single unit – the Madras European Regiment, later known as the Royal Madras Fusiliers – from 1799. Between 1824 and 1830, this was temporarily split into two battalions, before a new regiment of European infantry – the Madras Light Infantry – was created in 1839. A third regiment of European infantry was raised in 1853 with the denomination of the Madras Infantry. The artillery of the Madras Army continued its expansion after 1824, and by 1857 it mustered one brigade of horse artillery (with four European troops and two native troops), three battalions of European foot artillery (each with four companies) and one battalion of native foot artillery (with six companies). In addition, there were two companies of sappers that had been organized in 1831.

The original European garrison of Bombay consisted of four infantry companies, which were increased to eight by 1742, while the first artillery company was created in 1748. After the Seven Years' War, the existing infantry companies were consolidated into a single battalion, and by 1788 the European foot troops of Bombay consisted of two regiments. The artillery was increased to three companies in 1755, which were consolidated into a battalion in 1759. In Bombay, the European infantry, despite its

Officer (left) and private (right) of the Bengal Native Infantry in 1880. Until the Indian Mutiny, the native infantry corps raised by the British in India were usually dressed with uniforms of European cut that were extremely similar to those of the British Army's infantry, except for the headgear. After the Mutiny, new uniforms having the same basic features as the one shown here were introduced; these were used until the massive adoption of khaki during the late nineteenth century. (*ASKB Military Collection*)

Trooper of the Bengal Native Cavalry (left) and private of the Bengal Native Infantry (right) in 1880. Until the Indian Mutiny, the native cavalry corps raised by the British in India were usually dressed with uniforms in light dragoon style that were extremely similar to those of the British Army's light cavalry, except for the headgear. Following the Mutiny, new uniforms with the same basic features as that shown here were introduced. These were modelled on the dress worn by the Indian irregular cavalry before the Mutiny and comprised a comfortable kurta blouse and a coloured cummerbund. (*ASKB Military Collection*)

India 149

Private of the Bengal Native Infantry in 1888. In this case, the headgear is a simple pillbox cap rather than the usual turban. (*ASKB Military Collection*)

denomination, comprised several soldiers of mixed descent known as *topasses*. The Bombay Presidency was slower than the other two in assembling its independent companies of native infantry, and it was only during 1768 that the first two battalions of sepoys were created. These were increased to four in the following years. During the 1780s, the expansion of the native infantry continued, to the point that they came to comprise six battalions as well as two independent foot units: the Grenadier Battalion and the Marine Battalion. The former was an elite corps of heavy infantry,

Trooper of the Viceroy of India's Bodyguard. In 1947, this unit was transformed into the mounted guard of India's Prime Minister; it is still dressed with an elegant red uniform very similar to the one shown here.

while the latter was a naval infantry unit tasked with operating on the EIC's armed ships. In 1788, the six battalions of native infantry were augmented to twelve and assembled into two brigades, each having six battalions. In 1796, the existing native foot units were assembled into two-battalion regiments. By 1802, the single battalion of European artillery had been expanded to have seven companies. Prior to 1803, the Bombay Army did not have any permanent cavalry corps, the required mounted contingents provided by the Indian princedoms that were allies of the EIC. In 1803, the first troop of native cavalry was raised, followed by a second one in 1816; during 1817, these two troops were transformed into regiments. A third regiment of native light cavalry was formed in 1820. Like the Bengal Army, that of Bombay had some irregular native cavalry, which consisted of a single unit by 1824: the Poona Auxiliary Horse. In 1820, the European artillery of Bombay was restructured on two battalions of five companies; a first troop of horse artillery had been raised in 1811. By 1824, the native infantry consisted of twelve regiments, each having two battalions, but the European infantry mustered just one regiment – the Bombay European Regiment (later known as the Royal Bombay Fusiliers) – until a temporary second unit was raised between 1824 and 1829. In 1839, a new regiment of European infantry – the Bombay Light Infantry – was created. A third regiment of European infantry was raised in 1853, the Bombay Infantry. A single company of native pioneers existed in the Bombay Army since 1777, which was transformed into a company-sized Corps of Sappers and Miners in 1820. During 1826 and 1827, the first nine companies of native foot artillery were formed, being expanded to twelve during the following decades. In 1846, these were assembled into two battalions having six companies each. After 1839, the irregular cavalry of Bombay was expanded with the addition of three new corps: the Gujarat Irregular Horse, Scinde Irregular Horse and South Mahratta Horse. In 1844, the territory of the Bombay Presidency was significantly expanded with the annexation of Sind and Balochistan. These two regions were inhabited by warlike martial races, and their conquest permitted the formation of new military corps. By 1846, two battalions of Belooch native infantry had been raised, together with another regiment of Scinde Irregular Horse. Three new battalions of native infantry were also raised to garrison Sind. By 1857, the native infantry of the Bombay Army mustered thirty-one infantry battalions (the previous organization based on regiments having been abandoned), including the two autonomous ones recruited in Balochistan. These units were supplemented by eight Local Corps of irregular infantry created from 1825–1857. The artillery of the Bombay Army, by 1857, mustered one brigade of horse artillery (with four European troops, three of which had been raised between 1820 and 1824), two battalions of European foot artillery (each with four companies) and two battalions of native foot artillery (each with six

NCO of the 1st Regiment of Bengal Lancers (the former Skinner's Horse) in 1896. This unit received a very distinctive yellow uniform soon after its formation. (*ASKB Military Collection*)

companies). In addition, there were five companies of sappers that had been reorganized in 1830.

The Indian Mutiny, the greatest military uprising ever seen among the colonial troops of the British Empire, broke out in 1857. The rebellion involved a large portion of the EIC's native forces and came close to causing the total collapse of Britain's colonial presence in India. It was ignited by the diffusion of a false story related to the introduction of the new Pattern 1853 Enfield rifle, according to which the cartridges of the new weapon were greased with the fat of pigs (unclean to Muslims) and the fat of cows (holy to Hindus). The sepoys, upon learning that they would be required to bite off the end of the new cartridges before loading their rifles, feared that the British planned to Christianize them all, and began revolting against their white officers. The Indian Mutiny of 1857–1858 mostly affected the Bengal Army and was characterized by many atrocities, the mutinous sepoys being joined by increasing numbers of civilians who wanted to free their homeland from British control. The uprising forced the commanders of the Bengal Army to raise several new units from those

Trooper of the 1st Regiment of Bengal Lancers (the former Skinner's Horse) in 1900. After the Indian Mutiny, all the native cavalry units were progressively transformed into lancer corps. (*Colour plate by Patricio Greve Moller, copyright of Gabriele Esposito*)

native communities that remained loyal to the EIC – including the Sikhs from Punjab – in order to replace the many corps that had mutinied. The Sikhs contributed eighteen regiments of infantry and four of irregular cavalry. All the native cavalry regiments of the Bengal Army mutinied, together with most of the native infantry. As a result, four new cavalry regiments had to be raised from the European residents in Bengal. These and the four newly formed Sikh mounted regiments were supported by seventeen irregular cavalry corps that were formed by recruiting individuals who were still loyal to the British. Something similar happened for the infantry, with the formation of thirty new irregular corps. The Madras Army was not greatly affected by the Indian Mutiny, but its commanders were forced to disband four regiments of native cavalry and raise six new native foot units (which had a temporary nature and were tasked with performing garrison duties). Only two regiments of native infantry from the Bombay Army mutinied, these being disbanded. Several new corps were raised by the

Trooper of the 18th Regiment of Bengal Lancers in 1902. Each of the Indian cavalry regiments had the kurta blouse in a distinctive colour. (*ASKB Military Collection*)

Trooper of the 10th Regiment of Bengal Lancers in 1896. (*ASKB Military Collection*)

Trooper of the 2nd Regiment of Bengal Lancers in the early twentieth century. The white metal scales placed on the shoulders were typical of the Indian native cavalry's dress. (*ASKB Military Collection*)

Native officer of the Madras Native Infantry in 1880. (*ASKB Military Collection*)

Bombay Presidency during the Indian Mutiny: two regiments of regular native cavalry (known as the Central India Horse), six regiments of irregular native cavalry and eight regiments/battalions of regular native infantry (one of which was recruited from Balochistan). The Indian Mutiny came to an end in 1858 after the British government sent massive reinforcements to Bengal and thousands of mutineers were brutally executed. On 1 November 1858, Queen Victoria became the head of the government of India, which officially became part of the British Empire as a new colony. The glorious days of the East India Company – which had proved unable to stop the insurrection – were over and the colonial forces of India had to be completely reorganized. First of all, the EIC's artillery and sapper units were disbanded, except for five batteries that were attached to the Punjab Frontier Force and four batteries that were part of the semi-autonomous Hyderabad Contingent. The nine European infantry regiments of the three presidencies were all absorbed into the British Army: the Royal Bengal Fusiliers became the 101st Regiment of Foot, the Royal Madras Fusiliers was renamed the 102nd Regiment of Foot, the Royal Bombay Fusiliers became the 103rd Regiment of Foot, the Bengal Light Infantry received the denomination of the 104th Regiment of Foot, the Madras Light Infantry became the 105th Regiment of Foot, the Bombay Light Infantry was renamed the 106th Regiment of Foot, the Bengal Infantry became the 107th Regiment of Foot, the Madras Infantry became the 108th Regiment of Foot and the Bombay Infantry was

Private of the Madras Native Infantry in 1880.

thereafter called the 109th Regiment of Foot. The four European cavalry regiments formed in Bengal during the rebellion were consolidated into three units and were absorbed into the British Army as the 19th, 20th and 21st Hussars. By 1860, the native infantry of Bengal consisted of fifty-one regiments: twelve were units that had

not mutinied, fourteen were from the new Sikh units that had been formed during the rebellion and twenty-five were former irregular corps that had been raised to deal with the mutineers. The total number of native foot units was later reduced to forty-eight. The Bengal cavalry was rebuilt in 1860 from the irregular cavalry regiments raised during the Indian Mutiny and came to comprise nineteen regiments. In 1861, the four foot units of Gurkhas were separated from the rest of the Bengal native infantry and were assigned their own numbering, being supplemented by the addition of a new corps, always made up of Nepalese soldiers and known as Hazara Gurkhas, which had previously been part of the Punjab Frontier Force. Both the Sikh units of the Punjab Frontier Force and the Hyderabad Contingent were placed under the direct control of the British administration in India. The native infantry of Madras was brought back to its pre-war establishment in 1860, while the native cavalry of the presidency was reduced to just four regiments. The native infantry of Bombay was restructured on thirty regiments/battalions, three of which were recruited from Balochistan; most of the new foot units formed during the Indian Mutiny were disbanded. The native cavalry of the Bombay

NCO of the Madras Native Infantry in 1902, wearing the new khaki uniform. (*ASKB Military Collection*)

British officer of the 2nd Regiment of Madras Lancers in 1902. The British officers of the native cavalry, differently from the native officers, were not dressed like their men but wore lancer-style uniforms of European cut with white cork helmets. (*ASKB Military Collection*)

Trooper of the 3rd Regiment of Madras Lancers in 1902. (*ASKB Military Collection*)

Presidency augmented its pre-war establishment of just one regiment. As a result of the above organizational changes, by 1861 the colonial military forces of India comprised the following:

- The Viceroy of India's Bodyguard
- The Governor General of Bengal's Bodyguard (performing ceremonial duties)
- Forty-eight regiments of Bengal native infantry
- Five regiments of Gurkha light infantry
- Ten regiments of Sikh/Punjab infantry (four entirely made up of Sikhs, having their own numbering)
- Nineteen regiments of Bengal native cavalry
- The Guides of Punjab (a special frontier force, mostly made up of Sikhs)
- Five regiments of Punjab native cavalry
- The Governor General of Madras' Bodyguard (performing ceremonial duties)
- Forty-one regiments of Madras native infantry (three of which were later converted to pioneer corps)
- Six infantry regiments of the Hyderabad Contingent
- Four regiments of Madras native cavalry
- Four cavalry regiments of the Hyderabad Contingent
- The Governor General of Bombay's Bodyguard (performing ceremonial duties)
- Thirty regiments of Bombay native infantry (of which three were rifle corps and three were Belooch)
- Six regiments of Bombay native cavalry
- Two cavalry regiments of the Central India Horse

In addition to the above, there were the few native batteries of mountain artillery that were part of the Punjab Frontier Force, the number of which was progressively increased to ten. Between 1886 and 1895, the Gurkha light infantry saw a significant expansion too, with the formation of five new regiments. By the end of the century, it consisted of ten units numbered 1–10 and was separate from the rest of the native infantry raised in India. Most of the native cavalry regiments listed above were re-equipped with lances from 1864. In 1895, the military structure based on the existence of three autonomous presidencies was abolished, and in its place four new military commands were established in India: one for Bengal, Madras, Bombay and the North-Western Frontier. The North-West Frontier Command controlled the Sikh/Punjab military forces, including the elite Guides of Punjab, and was responsible for all the operations conducted on the frontier with Afghanistan. The Gurkha units remained

Private of the Bombay Native Infantry in 1902. The infantry units from Bombay that were converted into sapper corps continued to be dressed like the rest of the infantry. (*ASKB Military Collection*)

NCO of the Belooch Native Infantry in 1902. (*ASKB Military Collection*)

Officer of the 2nd Regiment of Bombay Lancers in 1890. (*ASKB Military Collection*)

part of the Bengal Command, but retained a high degree of autonomy. From 1890, some regiments of Madras native infantry assumed the denomination of Burma Infantry, since they were garrisoned in Burma on the north-eastern frontier of India. By 1893, the Burma Infantry comprised seven battalions, which were mostly recruited from Gurkhas and Sikhs. Meanwhile, from 1891, the number of Belooch regiments in the Bombay native infantry was increased from three to five. The Viceroy of India's Bodyguard formed after the Indian Mutiny was an elite cavalry regiment, whose members were chosen among the best elements of the various native cavalry corps. It did not perform only ceremonial duties (like the mounted bodyguards of the governor generals) and like the two independent regiments of Central India Horse and the Hyderabad Contingent was placed under the direct control of the British administration in India. In 1903, Lord Kitchener carried out a major reform of the Indian armed forces, with the objective of improving and modernizing its combat capabilities. The organization based on four military commands was cancelled and all the existing military corps were numbered in sequence. The infantry was structured on 126 regiments, not including the Gurkha ones: regiments numbered 1–48 came from Bengal, those numbered 51–59 came from Punjab, those numbered 61–93 came from Madras, those numbered 94–99 came from Hyderabad and those numbered 101–130 came from Bombay. As suggested by the above, four regimental numbers were left vacant. The cavalry was structured on thirty regiments plus the autonomous Viceroy of India's Bodyguard and Corps of Guides: regiments numbered 1–19 came

NCO of the 1st Regiment of Bombay Lancers in the 1880s. (*ASKB Military Collection*)

Trooper of the 1st Regiment of Bombay Lancers in the 1890s, with the new khaki uniform. (*ASKB Military Collection*)

from Bengal, those numbered 21–25 came from Punjab, those numbered 26–28 came from Madras, those numbered 31–37 came from Bombay, those numbered 20, 29 and 30 came from Hyderabad and those numbered 38–39 were the former Central India Horse. By 1908, Lord Kitchener had assembled all the units listed above into nine divisions of infantry and eight brigades of cavalry.

NCO of the 13th Regiment of Bombay Lancers in the 1890s. (*ASKB Military Collection*)

In March 1885, the Russian Army attacked Afghanistan and obtained a significant victory at Panjdeh on the ill-defined Russian-Afghan frontier. The British authorities in India, fearing that the Russians could continue their expansion in Asia by conquering the whole of Afghanistan before turning their attention to India, reinforced their forces in the Indian sub-continent by creating a reserve of approximately 20,000 native soldiers recruited from the armies of the Indian 'Native States'. As stated above, much of India was administered by semi-autonomous rulers during the colonial period, these vassals of the British having their own military forces, which were progressively westernized during the course of the nineteenth century.

NCO of the Indian mountain batteries in the late 1880s. Until the Indian Mutiny, the native artillery corps raised by the British in India were usually dressed with uniforms that were extremely similar to those of the Royal Artillery, except for the headgear. The horse artillery was dressed in light cavalry fashion. After the Mutiny, new uniforms like the one shown here were introduced for the few artillery units that continued to be raised in India.

The armies of the Native States, by 1885, were drilled and uniformed very similarly to the Indian colonial troops raised by the British, and thus potentially represented a significant military resource. The British selected 20,000 soldiers from the best elements of these autonomous native armies, who made up a reserve force known as Imperial Service Troops. These were trained by British instructors and re-equipped by

British officer of the Gurkha infantry from the 1890s. He is wearing a patrol jacket with black frontal frogging. (*ASKB Military Collection*)

Private of the Gurkha infantry from the 1890s. The headgear is a pillbox cap, which became distinctive of the Gurkhas.

India 169

Private of the Gurkha
infantry in 1902.
(*ASKB Military Collection*)

NCO of the Sikh infantry in the early twentieth century. (*ASKB Military Collection*)

Native officer of a mountain battery from the Punjab Frontier Force in 1902. (*ASKB Military Collection*)

India 171

Infantry NCO of the Sikh Corps of Guides in 1897. (*Colour plate by Patricio Greve Moller, copyright of Gabriele Esposito*)

Cavalry trooper of the Sikh Corps of Guides in the 1890s. (*ASKB Military Collection*)

the rulers of their home states. Until 1885, with the exception of the Hyderabad Contingent that has been discussed above, the princely armies of India mostly acted as police contingents tasked with keeping internal security in their home states and performing ceremonial duties. All this changed with the formation of the Imperial Service Troops, which over time significantly improved their combat capabilities. Specific training schools were established for the new reserve corps, which was to be mobilized in case of emergency. Furthermore, a special staff of British officers was formed to regularly inspect the Imperial Service Troops. This reserve force provided auxiliary contingents to the British during the world wars and ceased to exist only in 1947, when India became independent and all the Native States disappeared. The following is a list of the military contingents provided by each Native State for the formation of the Imperial Service Troops between 1885 and 1914:

Private of the Sikh infantry in the late 1880s, wearing khaki campaign dress. (*ASKB Military Collection*)

India 173

NCOs of the infantry (left) and the cavalry (right) from the Hyderabad Contingent in 1896. The armies of the Princely States of India were all dressed like the Indian native military units raised by the British after the end of the Indian Mutiny. (*ASKB Military Collection*)

Alwar: one lancer regiment, one infantry battalion.
Bahawalpur: one lancer regiment, one infantry battalion.
Baroda: one lancer regiment, one infantry battalion.
Bharatpur: one lancer regiment, one infantry battalion.
Bhavnagar: one lancer regiment.
Bhopal: one lancer regiment, one infantry battalion.
Bikaner: one camel corps, one infantry battalion.
Faridkot: one lancer troop, one infantry company.
Gwalior: three lancer regiments, two infantry battalions.
Hyderabad: two lancer regiments.
Indore: one lancer regiment.
Jammu and Kashmir: one lancer squadron, five infantry battalions, two artillery batteries.
Jind: one lancer squadron, one infantry regiment.
Jodhpur: two lancer regiments.
Junagadh: one lancer squadron.
Kapurthala: one lancer squadron, one infantry battalion.
Khairpur: one camel corps.
Malerkotla: one sapper company.
Mewar: one lancer regiment.
Mysore: one lancer regiment.
Nabha: one lancer squadron, one infantry battalion.
Nawanagar: one lancer squadron.
Patiala: one lancer regiment, two infantry battalions.
Rampur: one lancer squadron, one infantry battalion.
Sirmoor: two sapper companies.

Trumpeter of the Bikaner Camel Corps, one of the units that made up the Imperial Service Troops. (*ASKB Military Collection*)

Chapter 7

Asia

Ceylon

In 1796, the British seized the Dutch colony of Ceylon (present-day Sri Lanka), a large island off the southern coast of India. Similarly to what happened in South Africa, the Dutch military garrison of the island was transferred to British pay. This consisted of some independent infantry companies recruited from Malay soldiers, which were consolidated into a larger unit known as the 1st Ceylon Regiment from 1801. During the following year, another regiment of this kind was raised for service in Sri Lanka. In 1805, the 3rd Ceylon Regiment was created, followed by the 4th Regiment in 1810. The first unit organized by the British on Ceylon was the best of them, consisting of nine line companies and one rifle company, and was transformed into an elite light infantry corps in 1814 after receiving the new name of His Majesty's Malay Regiment. The 2nd Ceylon Regiment had the same internal establishment as the first, but was mostly made up of Sinhalese soldiers, for which reason it was also known as the Ceylon Native Infantry. The 3rd Ceylon Regiment was formed with soldiers recruited from East Africa (mostly ex-slaves), who had already been organized since 1803 into a small Caffre Corps. The latter was disbanded and absorbed into the new unit, which had an establishment of ten companies. The 4th Ceylon Regiment was also made up of black soldiers from East Africa, except for a single company that consisted of Malays. It was disbanded in 1815 and absorbed into the 3rd Ceylon Regiment. In October 1804, the British formed a corps of Ceylon Light Dragoons, which was mostly raised from sepoys serving in the Madras Army of the East India Company. This had an establishment of 130 men, forty of whom were British. Since 1801, the British had also raised three companies of gun lascars for service in Ceylon, native transporters who provided essential assistance to the Royal Artillery. Most of these soldiers came from Bengal. In 1804, three companies of pioneer lascars were formed. In 1817, the 3rd Ceylon Regiment was disbanded, followed by the 2nd Ceylon Regiment in 1821. The 1st Ceylon Regiment was transformed into a rifle corps in 1820 and assigned the new denomination of the Ceylon Rifle Regiment. This unit had a large establishment of sixteen companies, which were increased to twenty-two in 1847 when the regiment was required to send six of its companies to

Asia

Private of the 1st Ceylon Regiment in 1815. The green jacket is like that of the contemporary British Army's rifle units. (*Colour plate by Patricio Greve Moller, copyright of Gabriele Esposito*)

British officer of the Ceylon Rifle Regiment in the 1820s. (*ASKB Military Collection*)

Hong Kong. The various companies of the regiment were made up of Sinhalese, Malay, Indian and African soldiers, giving the corps a distinct multi-ethnic character. In 1854, the companies garrisoning Hong Kong were sent back to Ceylon and the establishment of the regiment was reduced to fourteen companies. Between 1869 and 1871, the number of companies was progressively reduced to eight, and the Ceylon Rifle Regiment was completely dissolved in 1874. The internal establishment of the Ceylon Light Dragoons was reduced in 1812 and they were transformed into a troop; two decades later, in 1832, the corps was completely disbanded, with just a handful of its members (two NCOs and ten troopers) retained in service to make up a new paramilitary unit known as Mounted Orderlies. In 1873, due to the disbandment of the Ceylon Rifle Regiment, the British colonists living in Ceylon raised a volunteer unit known as the Matale Rifle Volunteer Corps, which was tasked with policing the profitable plantations on the island but was decommissioned soon after its creation. It was only in 1881 that a new military corps was recruited on a local basis in Ceylon, when the Ceylon Light Infantry Volunteers

Private of the Ceylon Rifle Regiment from the early 1840s. (*Colour plate by Patricio Greve Moller, copyright of Gabriele Esposito*)

were formed. The new unit consisted of ten companies, whose members were mostly British or Eurasians. In 1888, a corps of Garrison Artillery Volunteers was created, which was followed by several other volunteer units. By 1905, in addition to the Ceylon Light Infantry Volunteers and Garrison Artillery Volunteers, the following colonial corps existed on the island: the Ceylon Planters Rifle Corps (a regiment made up of white planters), the Ceylon Mounted Rifles (a company that originated as a mounted detachment of the Ceylon Light Infantry Volunteers) and the Ceylon Engineers. In 1910, the various volunteer units became collectively known as the Ceylon Defence Force.

Burma

For most of the eighteenth century, the Burmese Empire was a leading military power in Indochina, fighting several bloody wars against the Thai state of Siam. The Burmese had ambitions to expand their territory towards the north-eastern regions of India and did not fear a military reaction by the East India Company. They could deploy a sizeable army that was well trained and partly equipped with modern firearms purchased from Britain's colonial rivals. By the beginning of the nineteenth century, Burmese expansion into the Indian regions of Manipur and Assam had created a long border between British India and the Burmese Empire. In 1822, the British began supporting Indian insurgents from Manipur and Assam who resented Burmese rule, providing them with weapons and supplies. The Burmese responded by launching small-scale incursions against the frontier areas of British territory. Tensions grew rapidly, to the point that the Burmese deployed most of their armed forces into Manipur and Assam in view of a direct confrontation with Britain. In September 1823, with war seeming inevitable, the Burmese occupied Shalpuri Island, near Chittagong, which had been claimed by the East India Company. The island's capture by Burmese soldiers led to the outbreak of the First Anglo-Burmese War. This formally began on 5 March 1824, after some border skirmishes between EIC soldiers and Burmese forces in Arakan. Britain was particularly worried by Burmese expansionism, especially because of the positive relations that existed between the Burmese court and France. Indeed, France hoped to exert an increasing influence over the Burmese Empire. The Bengal Presidency of the EIC was in search of new Asian markets where British products could be sold in great quantities, and Burma was a perfect target. The Burmese Army, at least on paper, was one of the largest and most effective native forces in Asia. For war with Britain, it mobilized 10,000 veteran infantry and 500 cavalry, who were commanded by experienced leaders. Burmese war plans were based on attacking the British in Arakan from the south-east and in

Cachar from the north-east. In the early phase of hostilities, the Burmese were able to push back the British forces facing them because they were familiar with fighting in the jungle environment of north-eastern India. The British moved very slowly across the dense woodlands of the theatre of operations, having only a limited knowledge of the local terrain. On 17 May 1824, they were defeated at the Battle of Ramu by the Burmese, who thereafter fought their way into the Bengal Presidency. At this point of the war, two Burmese columns joined forces and seemed ready to invade British Bengal. The EIC responded by sending all its warships to the Bengal coast and requesting the help of the British government. With the city of Calcutta threatened, the British assembled an elite expeditionary force of 10,000 men (5,000 British soldiers and 5,000 sepoys) for an attack on the Burmese mainland. The British expeditionary force consisted of seven regiments of foot from the British Army, one European infantry regiment from the Madras Army, twelve native infantry regiments from the Madras Army, three native infantry regiments from the Bengal Army, detachments of artillery and detachments of sappers. On 11 May 1824, British forces

Burmese auxiliary in British service from the 1820s. (*ASKB Military Collection*)

Private of the Sylhet Local Battalion in 1837. The uniform is practically identical to that of the Gurkha infantry. (*Colour plate by Patricio Greve Moller, copyright of Gabriele Esposito*)

entered the harbour of Rangoon, the Burmese capital, taking the defenders by surprise. They soon took up positions in the Shwedagon Pagoda compound, which they fortified, and from their new base they expelled the Burmese from Rangoon and obtained a series of minor victories. With a British army on their national soil, the Burmese had no choice but to suspend the invasion of Bengal. By November 1824, the Burmese had assembled 30,000 soldiers outside their capital in a bid to recapture it. They launched several violent frontal assaults on the British defensive positions, which were all repulsed with heavy losses. By the end of December, the Burmese only had 7,000 soldiers still alive and abandoned their attack on Rangoon.

In March 1825, the British attacked what remained of the Burmese forces at Danubyu, where the Burmese had built a fortified camp defended by 10,000 soldiers. On 1 April, after several weeks of intense fighting, the Burmese troops were crushed and their defensive positions destroyed. Meanwhile, in Bengal, the British launched a counter-offensive against the last Burmese troops that remained in the region. This was a complete success and led to the British occupation of the Arakan region. On 17 September 1825, an armistice of one month was concluded by the warring sides after the British had also expelled the Burmese from the border region of Assam. Hostilities resumed when the armistice expired and peace talks failed. In November 1825, the Burmese gathered all their remaining forces to fight a last battle against the British. The British attacked first on 1 December at Prome, the resulting battle ending in a great victory for the British and the Burmese then surrendering. In February 1826, the signing of the Treaty of Yandabo brought the First Anglo-Burmese War to an end. In accordance with the treaty, the Burmese Empire ceded to the British several border regions – Assam, Manipur, Arakan and Tenasserim – and paid a war indemnity of £1 million. The outcome of the First Anglo-Burmese War practically destroyed the finances of the Burmese Empire, but victory came at a high human cost for the British, who lost around 15,000 men, mostly due to tropical diseases. The loss of rich frontier territories was particularly humiliating for the Burmese, who fought another two wars against the British in 1852 and 1885. The Second Anglo-Burmese War of 1852–1853 was fought on a small scale and ended with the British annexing a large portion of Burmese territory known as Lower Burma (comprising the Irrawaddy Delta and the Burmese coastal regions located on the Gulf of Bengal). The Third Anglo-Burmese War of 1885 lasted for just a few weeks and resulted in the British annexation of Burma as a province of India. Some sporadic resistance to the British colonial rule continued until 1896, but from 1885 Burmese territory was firmly under British control.

After the First Anglo-Burmese War, the British stationed three locally raised units on the territories they had recently taken from Burma: the Rangpur Light Infantry

(a light infantry battalion formed in 1817 and renamed the 1st Assam Light Infantry in 1844), the Assam Sebundy Corps (eight companies of native irregulars formed in 1835 and renamed the 2nd Assam Light Infantry in 1844) and the Sylhet Local Battalion (ten companies of native irregulars formed in 1824). In 1861, the three units were transformed into native infantry regiments of the Bengal Army. By 1886, the original Assamese soldiers making up the three infantry corps had been completely replaced by Gurkhas and the three units assumed the new denomination of Gurkha Rifle Regiments. Their main task was patrolling the frontier dividing Bengal from Burma and keeping the peace among the warlike native tribes living on India's savage north-eastern border. Until 1903, the three regiments had their own small artillery detachments, since they were the only military corps specifically trained to operate on the wild terrain of Burma. From 1825, the British organized several irregular levies of native warriors in the frontier regions of Burma, in order to create some auxiliary contingents that could patrol the border areas. In 1861, two paramilitary corps of native police were formed from these levies: the Nowgong Frontier Police Battalion and North Cachar Hills Frontier Police Battalion. Another two battalions of Frontier

Burmese auxiliary in British service from the 1850s. (*ASKB Military Collection*)

Privates of the Burma Frontier Police (left) and Burma Military Police (right) in the 1880s.
(*Colour plate by Patricio Greve Moller, copyright of Gabriele Esposito*)

Police were later added to the existing two, so that in 1881 the new Assam Military Police could be formed with an establishment of four battalions. These had officers from India and were specialized in jungle warfare, their main task being to conduct counter-insurgency operations against Burmese resistance fighters. During the 1890s, a fifth battalion was added to the Assam Military Police and a new irregular corps – the Chin Levy – was raised. Following the Third Anglo-Burmese War and the British annexation of Burma, new battalions of the Burma Military Police were raised for service in mainland Burma. By 1937, the year during which Burma became an autonomous colony separate from India, the Burma Military Police deployed nine battalions that included significant numbers of Gurkhas.

Singapore, Malay and Borneo

In 1819, the British established a small trading post on Singapore, a small island located at the southern tip of the Malay Peninsula, which has always had great commercial importance due to its geographical position. Singapore controls the nearby straits that connect the Gulf of Bengal with the South China Sea. By exploiting the political weakness of the native states in the Malay Peninsula, which were formally vassals of Siam (modern Thailand), the British East India Company gradually penetrated into an area of the world that had been dominated by the Dutch until the beginning of the Napoleonic Wars. In 1790, the British had occupied the small island of Penang, then in 1824 they obtained the important coastal city of Malacca from the Dutch. During 1824, Singapore was officially transformed into a Crown Colony due to its great commercial importance. Two years later, in 1826, the British possessions in Malay – Penang, Singapore and Malacca – were united as the Straits Settlements. These were placed under the control of the EIC and soon flourished economically. In 1867, following the decline of the EIC, the Straits Settlements became a Crown Colony. Over time, the British exerted increasing political influence over the native princedoms of Malay, transforming all of them into vassal states. As a result, by the beginning of the twentieth century, the whole Malay Peninsula was under direct or indirect British control.

While the events described above took place in what later became known as British Malaya, the British started penetrating into the nearby large island of Borneo (located to the south-east of Singapore). In 1841, the Sultanate of Brunei, the major regional power of Borneo, ceded Sarawak in north-western Borneo to the British adventurer and former EIC member James Brooke in exchange for his military services against the pirates of Borneo. Brooke, who created his own dynasty of white rulers in Sarawak, established good relations with the British government but always preserved the autonomy of his small princedom. In 1846, the Sultanate of Brunei ceded the strategic island of Labuan on the northern coast of Borneo to the British, who transformed it into a Crown Colony during 1848. Like in the Malay Peninsula, the British soon started to exert increasing political influence over the native states of northern Borneo. By 1882, Sabah in north-eastern Borneo was transformed into a British protectorate. In 1890, Labuan and Sabah were united to form the new protectorate of British North Borneo. Sarawak remained an independent state until 1946, when it was finally annexed by Britain. In 1963, British Malaya, Singapore, British North Borneo and Sarawak all became independent from British colonial rule as the modern nation of Malaysia. In 1965, however, Singapore ceased to be part of Malaysia and became independent.

Private of the Malay Federated States Police Force in 1896.

The British formed a first locally raised unit in Malay only in 1933, the Malay Regiment, always fearing that giving weapons to the Malays – who were the most famous pirates in Asia – would cause trouble to their colonial administration. Like happened in India, however, the vassal states of the Malay Peninsula were permitted to maintain small princely armies that were tasked with performing police and ceremonial duties. One of these armies, that of the Sultanate of Johore, was even westernized along British lines during the late nineteenth century; by 1895, it consisted of 270 men assembled into one guard corps, one infantry company and one artillery battery. Another Malay state that regularized its military during the second half of the nineteenth century was the Sultanate of Perak, which created a paramilitary corps of policemen in 1873 by recruiting 110 retired Sikh sepoys. This unit, the Perak Police Force, was transformed into a British-controlled corps – the 1st Perak Sikh Battalion – during 1884. The latter gradually came to muster 200 Sikhs and 600 Malays. In 1896, the battalion assumed the new denomination of Malay States

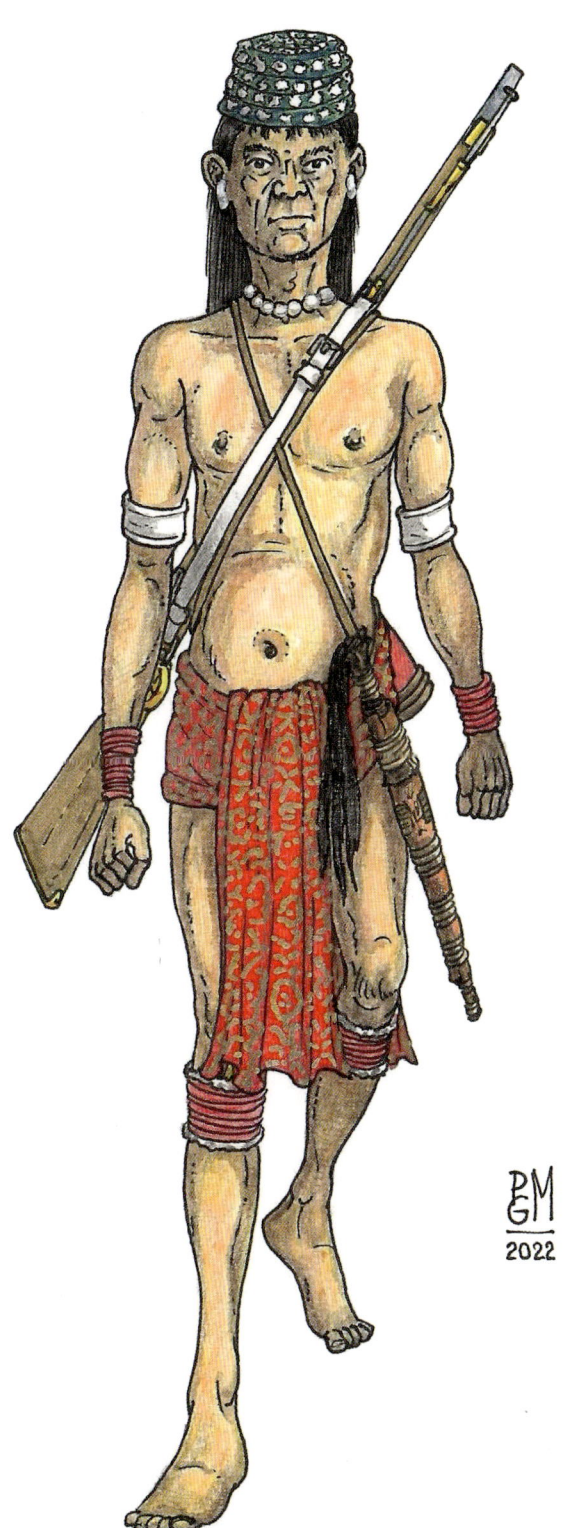

Private of the Sarawak Rangers in the early 1860s. He is wearing the traditional costume of the Iban warriors from Borneo who were recruited by James Brooke. (*Colour plate by Patricio Greve Moller, copyright of Gabriele Esposito*)

188 Queen Victoria's Colonial Troops, 1837–1901

Sikh private (left) and Chinese private (right) of the Hong Kong Police in the 1890s. The Hong Kong Regiment was dressed like the Sikh infantry units serving in India.

Guides, having transformed two of its eight companies into artillery units and received British officers. It was disbanded in 1919. From 1884, the Sultan of Perak also had a cavalry troop of Sikh bodyguards that acted as the sultan's mounted escort. Until 1914, the British regular garrison in Malay consisted of an Indian native infantry regiment, supported by detachments of the Royal Artillery and the Royal Engineers. From 1896, there was also a Federated States Police Force in Malay that consisted of around 2,150 militarized policemen. Sarawak had its own small and autonomous military force from 1862, which comprised the Sarawak Rangers. These were policemen recruited by James Brooke from former head-hunters or pirates of the Iban tribal communities. They were based in a number of forts constructed at strategic locations (such as river mouths) and fought in the jungle employing counter-insurgency methods. The Sarawak Rangers consisted of a single company with light equipment, losing their paramilitary nature in 1932. Singapore has long been inhabited by a large Chinese community, whose members were mostly merchants. However, the Chinese inhabitants of the island were divided by strong internal rivalries that frequently erupted into bloody riots. To deal with such security problems, the European residents of Singapore raised a volunteer military force in 1854 to keep law and order in the colony. This assumed the name of the Singapore Volunteer Rifle Corps and received official recognition from the British colonial authorities in 1857. It consisted of a single foot company, which was supported by a half-battery of artillery from 1868. It was disbanded in 1887, but the following year it was revived as the Singapore Volunteer Artillery Corps. During the 1890s, several new volunteer units – mostly made up of British and Eurasians – were created in Singapore. In 1901, these were reorganized together with the Singapore Volunteer Artillery Corps as the Singapore Volunteer Corps, which was structured on one company of European rifles, one company of European artillery, one corps of European engineers, one infantry company of Eurasians and one infantry company of Chinese. Singapore was always garrisoned by British regular detachments provided by the Indian native infantry regiments, as well as by sections of the Royal Artillery and the Royal Engineers. From 1881, the island also had a well-organized police force, which comprised two separate branches: one was made up of Sikhs from India and was tasked with preventing civilian unrest; the other consisted of Europeans and acted as a civilian police. The corps of Sikh policemen continued to exist in Singapore until 1942 and always performed very well.

China

Great Britain and the Qing Empire of China were at war from 1839–1842 – mostly for commercial reasons – in the First Opium War. This conflict ended in a severe defeat for the Chinese, who were obliged to open five of their major ports for international trade (including that of Shanghai) and were forced to cede the strategic island of Hong Kong to the British. The British soon transformed their new territorial possession in China into a major hub for international commerce, as they had done with Singapore. In 1843, Hong Kong became a Crown Colony, and in 1860 – following the Qing Empire's defeat in the Second Opium War fought against Britain and France – its territory was expanded with the addition of the southern Kowloon Peninsula. Located just north of Hong Kong island, this land was given in perpetual lease to the British by the Chinese government. In 1898, after signing a new convention with the Qing Empire, Britain obtained a further expansion of the Hong Kong colony's territory and thus could annex the whole Kowloon Peninsula as well as all the minor islands located around Hong Kong. From 1842, Hong Kong was garrisoned by detachments of British regular units due to its great strategic importance. In 1854, however, the local European inhabitants formed a volunteer corps that assumed the name of the Hong Kong Volunteers. This consisted of a single infantry company, which was disbanded soon after the military emergency caused by the Crimean War came to an end. In 1860, the unit was re-raised as a result of the Second Opium War, but in 1866 it was dissolved again. In 1878, the new Hong Kong Artillery and Rifle Volunteer Corps was created, which had one field battery and one infantry company. In 1906, a troop of cavalry was added to the unit's establishment before the corps received the new official denomination of the Hong Kong Defence Corps. During 1881, in order to have a reliable regular unit to serve in Hong Kong on a permanent basis, the British Army formed the Hong Kong Regiment, which was raised from Sikhs in India and had very high standards of service. It played a prominent role during the Boxer Rebellion of 1900–1901 before being disbanded in 1902 to cut costs. In 1908, to have some regular batteries of artillery that could serve permanently in Hong Kong and Singapore, a new unit known as the Hong Kong-Singapore Battalion of Royal Garrison Artillery was created within the British Army. This had five companies/batteries designed for coastal defence: three were garrisoned in Hong Kong, one in Singapore and one in Mauritius in the Indian Ocean. From 1842, Hong Kong also had a police force, which came to number around 600 men during the second half of the century; some 400 of them were Indians, most of whom had served in the native infantry of the Bombay Army. Over time, however, the number of locally recruited Chinese policemen increased significantly, especially after 300 new policemen were recruited following the Hong Kong colony's territorial expansion in 1898.

Trooper of the Mounted Rangers from the Shanghai Volunteer Corps in the 1860s. (*Colour plate by Patricio Greve Moller, copyright of Gabriele Esposito*)

After its opening to international commerce in 1842, the major city of Shanghai started to be inhabited by a sizeable European community that was mostly made up of merchants. In order to ensure the security of their growing community, these Europeans decided to form a volunteer military unit in April 1853. This, known as the Shanghai Volunteer Corps, always comprised significant numbers of British. Initially, it consisted of just 150 volunteers who were assembled into three small companies of fifty men each. The Shanghai Volunteer Corps had a quite turbulent history: disbanded in 1855, it was re-raised in 1860 (due to the Second Opium War) only to be disbanded again in 1867. Finally, in 1870, it was re-formed on a permanent basis and continued to exist until 1939. In 1862, the corps was expanded with the addition of fifty infantrymen and the formation of two sub-units: one cavalry troop (Mounted Rangers) and one half-battery of artillery. Over time, with the expansion of the European community in Shanghai, the Shanghai Volunteer Corps was greatly enlarged with the creation of new sub-units that were formed on a national basis. By 1873, the British element consisted of three infantry companies with fifty men each, the troop of Mounted Rangers and a small artillery detachment. The Shanghai Volunteer Corps was never part of the British colonial units, but it had many elements in common with them – uniforms and equipment, for example – since the majority of its members were British citizens. In 1860, during the Second Opium War, the British

NCO of the Canton Coolie Corps in 1860. The number of the company is reproduced on the front of the uniform. (*Colour plate by Patricio Greve Moller, copyright of Gabriele Esposito*)

Private of the Wei-Hai-Wei Regiment in 1900, wearing the wide-brimmed straw hat and khaki uniform that were peculiar of this corps. (*Colour plate by Patricio Greve Moller, copyright of Gabriele Esposito*)

military commanders operating in China raised a unit of coolies (manual workers specialized in transporting goods) from the Hakka people. The regiment, known as the Canton Coolie Corps, consisted of ten companies, each of which was assigned to a different British regular unit in order to carry their materials. At the end of hostilities there were proposals to retain the corps as part of Hong Kong's garrison, but these came to nothing and the regiment was disbanded. In 1898, the small coastal city of Wei-Hai-Wei, located in the Shandong province of China, was leased to Britain by the Qing government. The British soon transformed the city into a major port of northern China, which acted as the summer anchorage of the Royal Navy's China Station and thus acquired a significant military importance. In order to protect their new territorial possession, the British authorities raised a Chinese native infantry regiment from the inhabitants of the Shandong province. This, known as the Wei-Hai-Wei Regiment or 1st Chinese Regiment, had British officers and consisted of eight companies. It played a significant role during the Boxer Rebellion of 1900–1901 before being reduced to just four companies and then being disbanded in 1906 to cut costs. Several former members of the regiment became part of the small constabulary force that garrisoned British Wei-Hai-Wei until 1930.

Aden Troop

On 18 January 1839, the British East India Company captured the important port of Aden in present-day Yemen, with the intention of establishing a supply base on the southern coastline of the Arabian Peninsula and stopping the frequent attacks by Arab pirates directed against British shipping to India. The city of Aden, which became subordinate to the Bombay Presidency before gaining the status of Crown Colony in 1937, was located half-way along the flourishing commercial routes that connected Egypt with India across the Red Sea. For this reason, it became increasingly important from a strategic point of view after the opening of the Suez Canal. With the progress of time, the British started to exert an increasing political influence over the Arab communities living in the interior areas that surrounded Aden. Consequently, in 1873, these areas were organized as the Aden Protectorate. Aden was a very important base for the Royal Navy from the outset (it was home to the Red Sea Squadron) and always had a significant regular garrison provided by the native colonial units of India. The British formed their first locally raised colonial corps in Aden only in 1917 – the Aden Rifles – and by 1914 the garrison of Yemen comprised just British or Indian military units. It was known as the Aden Brigade and comprised one British infantry battalion, one Indian infantry battalion and one Indian cavalry troop (called the Aden Troop, which was formed in 1867 and recruited from Balochistan).

Asia 195

Trooper of the Aden Troop in the early twentieth century. The khaki uniform is identical to that worn by the contemporary Indian cavalry units. (*ASKB Military Collection*)

Chapter 8

Africa

Western Africa

At the beginning of the nineteenth century, Great Britain had only a few colonial possessions of modest dimensions in Africa. These were located in the Gulf of Guinea in Western Africa and consisted of small footholds extending along the coastline. British possessions included portions of present-day Gambia, Ghana (at the time known as Gold Coast) and Sierra Leone. It was in the latter territory that the British had their main base of Freetown. In August 1800, the British authorities raised a regiment for the defence of their West African possessions, which was known as Fraser's Corps of Infantry from the name of its commander. Since no British soldiers wanted to serve in such dangerous colonial outposts, the new infantry unit had to be raised as a penal corps made up of deserters and condemned servicemen who had no choice but to join the regiment in order to regain their freedom. Once in Africa, the unit – originally consisting of two companies – was enlarged with the inclusion of local black recruits and participated in several military operations conducted against the French colony of Senegal. In 1804, the regiment (now structured on ten companies) received the new denomination of the Royal African Corps. Two years later, some of its men were detached to form a new unit that was to serve in the West Indies, the Royal West India Rangers. In 1807, the corps changed its name again, becoming the Royal York Rangers. During that same year, some of its men were detached to form another new unit to serve in the West Indies. This was called the Royal York Rangers, with the original corps of that name in Western Africa going back to its previous denomination of the Royal African Corps. From 1810, the latter was permitted to recruit significant numbers of black soldiers and thus gradually abandoned its original character of penal corps. In 1817, six companies of the Royal African Corps were sent to South Africa, where they were disbanded in 1821; the four companies remaining in Western Africa were reduced to a single one that assumed the denomination of the Royal African Colonial Light Infantry in 1821. This ceased to accept white individuals in its ranks in 1830 and continued to exist until 1840, when it contributed to the formation of the new 3rd West India Regiment. As we have seen in a previous chapter, since 1818 the British colonial possessions in Western Africa started to be garrisoned by detachments of the West India Regiments.

In the middle of the Atlantic Ocean, not far from the coast of Western Africa, Britain controlled the small island of St Helena, which in addition to being important due to its geographical position, was the isolated place where Napoleon spent the years of his exile from 1815–1821. Until 1836, St Helena was under the control of the East India Company and was garrisoned by two small regular military units: the St Helena Infantry Regiment and the St Helena Artillery Regiment. These were supported by four companies of militia, two of which were recruited from free blacks (the other two mostly consisted of veterans who had served in the EIC's regular corps). Following the transformation of St Helena into a Crown Colony, both the regular units of the EIC that were stationed on the island were disbanded. They were soon replaced by regular detachments provided by the British Army, which included small artillery and engineer elements. In 1842, bearing in mind St Helena's great importance as a naval base in the Atlantic, the British government decided to form a new infantry unit – Her Majesty's St Helena Regiment –

NCO of the Royal African Corps in 1815. (*Colour plate by Patricio Greve Moller, copyright of Gabriele Esposito*)

to garrison the island. The new corps consisted of just five companies and was mostly made up of volunteers from other foot regiments who were experienced soldiers of good conduct. Her Majesty's St Helena Regiment was disbanded in 1863 after two decades of service. During the second half of the nineteenth century, due to the presence of the British regular garrison, the militia of St Helena entered a long period of decay. In 1897, a small volunteer corps – the St Helena Volunteer Sharpshooters, consisting of a single light infantry company – was created on the island but ceased to exist in 1907.

In 1853, the British created their first locally raised colonial military unit in Western Africa, the Gold Coast Corps. This consisted of a single company that was tasked with garrisoning the forts located in present-day Ghana and assumed the new denomination of the Gold Coast Artillery Corps in 1857. In 1861, the British started penetrating into the territory of Nigeria, annexing the port of Lagos. However, this did not change the military situation in the area as the British possessions in Western Africa continued to be garrisoned by detachments of the West India Regiments. In 1862, the Gold Coast Artillery Corps, which had been expanded to comprise two companies, mutinied and was disbanded. From the 1820s, the British troops stationed in Western Africa started to face the powerful Ashanti Empire, one of the main regional powers of the Gulf of Guinea, which vehemently opposed the progressive British colonization of Western Africa. The Ashanti forces were equipped with significant numbers of modern firearms and were used to fighting in the dense forests that covered most of their homeland. They thus proved to be a fierce enemy of the West India Regiments, which experienced serious difficulties in dealing with them during the 1860s. In 1872, Britain purchased from the Netherlands the Dutch colonial outposts located on the coast of Western Africa. This led to the outbreak of a major war with the Ashanti Empire, which took place from 1873–1874 and caused serious losses to the British. To deal with the threat of the warlike Ashanti communities, the British raised various temporary levies of native auxiliaries as well as small volunteer corps made up of the few white settlers living in Western Africa. After the Ashanti Empire was defeated, the best elements of the new locally raised auxiliary corps were kept in service and organized as an infantry battalion named the Gold Coast Constabulary. The 1880s saw the progressive transformation of Nigeria into a British protectorate, which led to the formation of the Niger Coast Protectorate Force in 1893. This comprised an infantry battalion and was supported by the Lagos Constabulary, a paramilitary police corps created by the British in 1873 and recruited from the Hausa natives who were loyal to the Crown. In 1886, a Royal Niger Company Constabulary was formed in northern Nigeria, followed

Private of the Gold Coast Constabulary (left), NCO of the Gold Coast Constabulary (centre) and private of the Sierra Leone Frontier Force (right) in the 1890s. (*ASKB Military Collection*)

in 1890 by the Sierra Leone Frontier Police, which was soon expanded to comprise five companies.

The success of the various paramilitary constabularies created in Western Africa since 1873 convinced the British government to raise some proper military corps from that part of its colonial empire. As a result, in 1898, the West Africa Regiment was formed in Sierra Leone with an establishment of twelve companies. During 1899, using the Royal Niger Company Constabulary as its cadre, the West African Frontier Force was created. This consisted of two infantry battalions, two artillery batteries, one mounted infantry company and one engineer company. In 1901, following the suppression of the last major uprising of the Ashanti communities, the various paramilitary constabularies in British Western Africa were reorganized as proper

NCO (left) and drummer (right) of the Lagos Constabulary in the 1890s. (*ASKB Military Collection*)

military units: what remained of the Royal Niger Company Constabulary was transformed into the Northern Nigeria Regiment with two battalions; the Lagos Constabulary became the Lagos Battalion; the Niger Coast Protectorate Force was made into the Calabar Battalion; the Gold Coast Constabulary became the Gold Coast Regiment with two battalions; and the Sierra Leone Frontier Police was transformed into the Sierra Leone Battalion. All these units became part of the West African Frontier Force, with the Northern Nigeria Regiment, the Lagos Battalion, the Calabar Battalion and the Gold Coast Regiment all having two artillery batteries each. In 1902, following the British pacification of Gambia, a new infantry corps – known as the Gambia Company – was raised as part of the West African Frontier Force. In 1906, the Calabar Battalion and the Lagos Battalion were renamed – respectively – as the 1st Southern Nigeria Regiment and 2nd Southern Nigeria Regiment. They were amalgamated during 1911. In 1914, all the units raised from Nigeria were brought together to form a single Nigeria Regiment that mustered five battalions. As a

Private of the Nigeria Regiment in 1914. As shown here, most of the colonial units raised in Western Africa were dressed in Zouave-style like the West India Regiments. (*Colour plate by Patricio Greve Moller, copyright of Gabriele Esposito*)

result, by the beginning of the First World War, the West African Frontier Force consisted of five battalions of the Nigeria Regiment, one battalion from the Gold Coast (the other had been disbanded in 1907), one battalion from Sierra Leone and the Gambia Company. The West Africa Regiment, formed in 1898, continued to exist as an autonomous corps – which was not part of the West African Frontier Force – until being dissolved in 1928.

Central Africa

The British started their colonization of Central Africa by focusing on two areas located north of South Africa and south of Kenya: Nyasaland (modern Malawi) and Rhodesia (modern Zimbabwe). In 1891, Nyasaland formally became part of Great Britain's sphere of influence and assumed the denomination of the British Central African Protectorate. Initially, this had some small irregular forces that were known as the Indian Contingent since they comprised a number of Sikh soldiers recruited from India. These mostly acted as NCOs, while privates could be local African recruits or Arab mercenaries from Zanzibar. In 1896, the Indian Contingent was transformed into a regular military force called the Central African Rifles, which consisted of a battalion with six companies. In 1898, it became known as the 1st Central African Rifles, with a new battalion of the same kind, the 2nd Central African Rifles, also being raised. The 2nd Battalion was sent to Mauritius to act as the local garrison. In 1900, the two battalions were assembled together as the Central African Regiment. In 1890, the British South Africa Company, guided by Cecil Rhodes, began colonizing the southern part of Rhodesia. To garrison the newly acquired territories, the few British settlers raised a paramilitary Pioneer Column with two troops of mounted infantry and one company of artillery. The British South Africa Company also had its own police corps, which consisted of around 200 white individuals. By 1891, both the Pioneer Column and the British South Africa Company Police had been disbanded. These were replaced by a corps of volunteers – the Mashonaland Horse – and a new police unit called the Mashonaland Mounted Police. Rhodesia was inhabited by significant numbers of Boers from the beginning, and thus an irregular Burgher Force consisting of commandos was soon raised on its territory. In 1893, the territory of Matabeleland was also annexed to Rhodesia and a new police corps, the Matabeleland Mounted Police, was formed. This was supported from the start by a native police force, the Matabeleland Native Police. Meanwhile, the white settlers of Rhodesia organized a new volunteer corps called the Rhodesia Horse that could be mobilized in case of need. In 1896, the Mashonaland Mounted Police and Matabeleland Mounted Police were merged to create the Rhodesia Mounted

Police. The Rhodesia Horse was enlarged and assumed the new denomination of the Southern Rhodesian Volunteers. In 1899, to support Britain in its war against the Boers of South Africa, a Rhodesia Regiment of volunteer mounted infantry was created, but this new corps was disbanded in 1900. During the 1890s, the British started penetrating into the northern part of Rhodesia and new paramilitary units were formed: the North-Eastern Rhodesian Constabulary and Barotse Native Police. These were amalgamated in 1911 as the Northern Rhodesian Police, a force of native policemen commanded by white officers and NCOs. In 1901, the Central African Regiment from Nyasaland was absorbed into the King's African Rifles of Eastern Africa (see below for more details).

Eastern Africa

At the beginning of the nineteenth century, the dominant military power of Eastern Africa was the Arab Sultanate of Oman, in the south-western part of the Arabian Peninsula. Oman had long been a significant naval and commercial power, controlling large parts of Eastern Africa's coastline as well as the strategically important island of Zanzibar. Located near the mainland of present-day Tanzania, Zanzibar was the most important commercial centre in Eastern Africa and was the capital of the Sultanate of Oman from 1840. By 1870, Oman had an army of around 2,750 semi-regular soldiers, who mostly acted as policemen and were all mercenaries from Balochistan in India or the Swahili communities of Eastern Africa. Oman's few artillerymen were Turks from the Ottoman Empire. The British tried to limit the power of the Sultanate of Oman during the 1870s as they wanted to transform it into a protectorate. They restricted as much as possible the slave trade in Eastern Africa – which made Oman very rich – and sponsored the reorganization of the sultanate's armed forces along westernized lines. By 1880, under the guidance of British instructors, the army of Oman had been re-equipped with modern British weapons and consisted of 1,300 well-drilled regulars. In 1890, Britain declared its protectorate over Zanzibar. By that time, the forces of Oman stationed on the island consisted of 860 men assembled into twelve companies, who were all loyal to their British instructors. From 1895, hoping to limit the growing British influence over Zanzibar, the Sultan of Oman started raising a new private army that comprised a bodyguard made up of individuals with strong anti-British sentiments. These were, in most cases, black slaves commanded by Swahili mercenary officers. In 1896, the 1,200 guards of the sultan organized a major revolt against the British, counting on the diplomatic support of Germany. However, the rebellion was quickly crushed by the regular forces of Zanzibar (which sided with the British) and a landing party from the Royal Navy. Until 1906, the

Privates of the 3rd Battalion of the King's African Rifles (left) and the 4th Battalion of the King's African Rifles (right) in 1914. The 3rd Battalion was the former East Africa Rifles from Kenya, while the 4th Battalion was the former Uganda Rifles. (*Colour plate by Patricio Greve Moller, copyright of Gabriele Esposito*)

battalion-sized regular troops of Zanzibar continued to garrison their island on behalf of the British, but during that year they were disbanded and replaced by a contingent provided by the King's African Rifles of Eastern Africa. The latter was supported, after 1911, by a Zanzibar Armed Constabulary.

In 1888, the British East African Company was created with the objective of colonizing the interior of Eastern Africa, notably the territories of Kenya and Uganda that had already been visited by British explorers. Until 1895, the British East African Company deployed only small numbers of irregular mercenaries who were, in most cases, from Zanzibar or Somalia. In 1895, however, the territory of modern Kenya came under the direct control of the Crown and became known as the British East African Protectorate. The irregulars who had been at the service of the British East African Company were reorganized as the East Africa Rifles, which by 1898 consisted of five Sudanese companies and three Swahili companies plus an autonomous Indian Contingent of 300 Indian soldiers from the Bombay Army. In 1900, the Indian Contingent was dissolved and replaced by a new Swahili company. The British East African Company started penetrating into Uganda from 1889, and in 1891 it contracted 600 Sudanese soldiers who had previously been in Egyptian service

NCO of the Somaliland Camel Corps in 1914. (*Colour plate by Patricio Greve Moller, copyright of Gabriele Esposito*)

to garrison the newly acquired territories. In 1895, after Uganda came under the control of the Crown, these Sudanese troops were given a regular structure with eight companies and became the Uganda Rifles. They were reorganized in 1898 following a mutiny and were progressively expanded; by 1900 they consisted of eighteen companies, which included 400 Indian soldiers from Balochistan. In 1901, the East Africa Rifles, Uganda Rifles and Central African Regiment were merged to form the King's African Rifles, which was modelled on the West Africa Frontier Force and had six battalions, formed respectively from the former 1st Central African Rifles, 2nd Central African Rifles, East Africa Rifles, Uganda Rifles, Indian Contingent of the East Africa Rifles and Somali Levies (see below for more details). The 5th Battalion was disbanded in 1905, followed by the 2nd Battalion and 6th Battalion during 1911. Consequently, by 1914, the East Africa Rifles consisted of just three battalions (one each from Nyasaland, Kenya and Uganda) plus one battery of camel artillery. Britain established control over the north-western coastline of Somalia in 1884, when the small protectorate of British Somaliland was created. This was important for British interests, since it was located in front of Aden and with the latter controlled southern access to the Red Sea. Initially, the new protectorate was garrisoned by just 150 locally raised auxiliaries of the Coast Police, but the ascendancy of an extremist Muslim leader known as the Mad Mullah convinced the British to raise the Somali Levies, with 1,000 infantry and 500 mounted infantry. As noted above, these became part of the King's African Rifles before being disbanded in 1911. During 1911, a Camel Constabulary was raised in British Somaliland, which from 1914 was known as the Somaliland Camel Corps.

Egypt and Sudan

The political process that led to the transformation of Egypt from a semi-autonomous vassal state of the Ottoman Empire to a British protectorate was a quite rapid one. In 1881, an ambitious officer of the Egyptian Army, Arabi Pasha, mutinied against the government of his country and mounted a coup against the ruling Khedive (Governor) Tewfik Pasha. Arabi Pasha considered the Egyptian government too weak to counter the expansionist ambitions of Britain and France in northern Africa, but he also had deep anti-European and anti-Christian feelings. During the civil war that followed the uprising of Arabi Pasha, both Britain and France supported the Khedive, over whom they exerted strong diplomatic influence. Fearing that their citizens living in Egypt could be killed or harmed by Arabi Pasha's troops, the two European powers sent warships off the coast of Alexandria on 20 May 1882. A few weeks later, an anti-Christian riot took place in the port city, which resulted in the killing of fifty European civilians. At this point, Britain decided to intervene in the Egyptian civil war, aiming to defeat Arabi Pasha and transform Egypt into a protectorate. The French, who would benefit very little from an invasion of Egypt, did not join the British endeavour. The inauguration of the strategic Suez Canal in 1869 had transformed Egypt into the most important African country, especially from a British point of view. Britain was determined to use the Suez Canal to connect more rapidly and effectively their vast colonial possessions in India with the motherland. The British had invested substantial sums of money in Egypt during the 1870s and

Egyptian infantryman guarding a Krupp field piece in 1881; he is wearing white summer dress with red fez having a black tassel.

could not tolerate the country existing in a state of anarchy due to the ongoing civil war. On 11 July 1882, the British fleet started bombarding Alexandria, which had been heavily fortified by Arabi Pasha during the previous weeks. The bombardment was very heavy, destroying much of the city after starting numerous fires. Hundreds of civilians died, especially after Egyptian troops left the city. Alexandria was quickly occupied by a landing force from the British ships, which restored order in the city after some hours of unrest with lootings and violence.

Despite having lost Alexandria, Arabi Pasha continued his resistance against the British, recruiting more troops. He could count on the unconditional support of the Egyptian population and controlled most of Egypt's regular forces. The British launched a probing attack against the Egyptian positions at Kafr El Dawwar in a bid to reach Cairo, but found the Egyptian defences too strong for a swift breakthrough. As a result, in August 1882, the British government decided to assemble a large expeditionary force to invade the Suez Canal area. This comprised 40,000 soldiers and was commanded by General Wolseley. On 5 August, having landed in Alexandria, the British invasion force attacked the Egyptian lines at Kafr El Dawwar. The British were again forced back after a probing attack, realizing that a major assault was needed to defeat the Egyptian forces deployed there. The original British plan for reaching Cairo from Alexandria thus had to be abandoned. At this point of the campaign, Wolseley decided to use the Suez Canal to outflank the Egyptian positions. On 20 August, the British troops transported on the Suez Canal disembarked at Ismailia and occupied it without encountering resistance. A few days later, on 26 August, the British troops met the enemy at the Kassassin lock. Despite being outnumbered by Arabi Pasha's men, they repulsed all their assaults and forced the Egyptians to fall back with heavy casualties. The whole British expeditionary force then moved to Kassassin, where it started to prepare for a pitched battle with the Egyptians. Arabi Pasha, determined to defend his capital of Cairo from the British, had his main force dug in at Tell El Kebir, north of the railway and canal that linked Ismailia with Cairo. The Egyptian Army deployed at Tell El Kebir consisted of 18,000 soldiers equipped with modern rifles and sixty pieces of artillery, meaning that in a defensive battle it had a good chance of stopping the British assault. Wolseley, having determined that the Egyptians did not have outposts in front of their positions at night, saw that it was possible for an attacking force to approach the enemy defences under cover of darkness. The British troops thus moved close to the Egyptian positions by night and attacked frontally at dawn on 13 September 1882. They did not achieve total surprise, however, with the infantry and artillery defending the Egyptian redoubts opening fire when the attackers were some 550 metres from them. Nevertheless, the Egyptian fire proved ineffective and failed to halt the advance of the British. Despite suffering some losses, the British seized the redoubts after a short but violent hand-to-hand struggle. The Egyptians lost around 2,000 men and were completely routed. Soon after the battle, the British troops captured Cairo without meeting further serious resistance, the Egyptian capital having been left undefended. With the defeat of Arabi Pasha, who fled into exile, the ruling Khedive was formally restored by the British, with Egypt transformed into a protectorate of Great Britain. Thanks to its victory, the British could start exerting direct control over the Suez Canal and colonizing the vast region of Sudan with Egyptian support.

By the time of the British invasion in 1882, the Egyptian Army comprised eight regiments of infantry (six made up of Egyptians and two of Sudanese), three regiments of cavalry, two regiments of field artillery, three regiments of coastal artillery and one company of engineers. These regular forces were supplemented by large numbers of irregulars, who mostly consisted of foreign mercenaries tasked with garrisoning the territories controlled by Egypt in Sudan. The bands of irregulars – the equivalent of the bashi-bazouks in Ottoman service – were made up of Turks, Albanians, Circassians and Sudanese. The Egyptians had sent a large military expedition to Sudan in 1871, which was commanded by the British General Baker and annexed to Egypt a vast area of Sudan that had previously mostly remained independent. In 1875, having already established military garrisons in a few coastal cities of present-day Eritrea, the Egyptian government sent another military expedition to Abyssinia (modern Ethiopia) with the objective of conquering it. The Egyptians had ambitions to complete their conquest of Sudan and obtain control over most of Eastern Africa in order to dominate the Red Sea. The expedition against Abyssinia, however, ended in dismal failure, the Egyptian Army being massacred by Ethiopian tribal forces. The Egyptian Army of 1882 was, at least on paper, an impressive military force. It could count on the presence of several foreign instructors (mostly British professionals, but also veterans of the US Civil War) and followed the most modern military regulations of the time (those of the Prussian Army for the infantry and the French Army for the artillery). The infantry regiments each had three battalions, and a single battalion consisted of eight companies. Meanwhile, the cavalry regiments had six squadrons each, the field artillery regiments each had four foot batteries and two mounted batteries, and the coastal artillery regiments had six static batteries each. The regular soldiers were raised by conscription and served for different lengths of time according to their branch of service: five years for infantrymen, six years for cavalrymen and seven years for artillerymen. By paying a special tax, each conscript could reduce his period of service to just one year. After completing his service in the regular army, a conscript became part of the Army Reserve for seven years. The Reserve could be mobilized quite rapidly in case of military emergency and consisted

Sudanese infantryman in 1896. The brown sweater was very popular for campaign use. (*Colour plate by Patricio Greve Moller, copyright of Gabriele Esposito*)

of around 30,000 men. The Christians living in the large urban centres of Alexandria and Cairo were exempt from military service. The regulars and Army Reserve, in addition to the irregulars described above, could also count on the support of a highly militarized gendarmerie force. When hostilities with Britain began in 1882, Arabi Pasha mobilized the Army Reserve and thus was able to deploy a total of sixty infantry battalions for the campaign.

Following the transformation of Egypt into a British protectorate, the Egyptian Army was completely reorganized. Its new commander was Major General Wood, a distinguished member of the British Army. Wood, together with a staff of twenty-six experienced instructors provided by the British Army, restructured the Egyptian Army during 1883. The size of the Egyptian armed forces was significantly reduced, but their quality improved, consisting of the following: two brigades of infantry, both with four battalions of four companies; one regiment of cavalry with four squadrons; and one detachment of field artillery with four batteries. It became apparent, however, that these forces were too small to control the whole of Egypt, as well as Sudan. From 1880, Sudan was ruled by Charles George Gordon, an experienced British general who had been chosen by the Egyptian government as the governor of its Sudanese territories. Gordon worked hard to stabilize the Egyptian presence in Sudan and deal with the illegal activities of local slave-traders, but could not prevent the ascendancy of the Mahdist State of Sudan. This was ruled by a charismatic religious leader named Muhammad Ahmad, who wanted to restore the original purity of Islam in Sudan by expelling the Egyptians once and for all. In 1881, Muhammad Ahmad proclaimed himself the Mahdi (the 'expected one') and launched a holy war against the foreigners living in Sudan. His religious fundamentalism soon transformed Sudanese society and caused serious trouble for the Egyptian authorities. The small Egyptian garrisons around Sudan were all destroyed by the Mahdists, leaving only the larger one in Khartoum, the Sudanese capital located on the Nile. To reconquer Sudan and counter the activities of the Mahdists, the Egyptian government assembled an expeditionary force commanded by the British General Hicks. This comprised four temporary infantry regiments with three battalions each, one mixed cavalry and artillery regiment equipped with twenty field pieces, and five bands of irregular auxiliaries. Hicks's expeditionary force, having wandered without water across the Sudanese desert for several days, was ambushed and completely destroyed by the Mahdist insurgents in 1883.

Following these events, with British approval, the Egyptian authorities began expanding their regular army with the formation of several new units. By 1886, the Egyptian Army consisted of the following corps: ten battalions of infantry, one regiment of cavalry, five batteries of artillery and one camel corps. The infantry battalions had four companies each; the two new ones, the 9th and 10th, were not part of the two existing brigades and were entirely recruited from Sudanese. The cavalry regiment had four squadrons, while the artillery consisted of two field batteries, two mountain batteries and one depot battery. One field battery and one mountain battery had six guns each, while the remaining two had four guns each. The camel corps, being a squadron with three companies of infantrymen mounted on dromedaries, was specifically created to fight against the Mahdists in the desert of Sudan. All the various Egyptian units comprised a number of British senior officers, so the military influence exerted on the Egyptian Army by the British was very strong. By early 1884, the Egyptian situation in Sudan was desperate, the Mahdists having conquered the whole country except for the city of Khartoum, where the Egyptian garrison was besieged. General Gordon did his best to continue resisting and repulsed several Mahdist attacks against his positions. He improved the fortifications of Khartoum and obtained some minor successes, but it became apparent that his remaining troops would be destroyed if no relief expedition was sent from Egypt. Since Gordon was an extremely popular figure in his homeland and since Egypt could not afford to lose Sudan, the British government finally decided to assemble a relief expedition to save the Sudanese capital from being captured by the Islamist insurgents. The Nile Expedition, under the command of the experienced General Wolseley, tried to reach Khartoum by steaming up the Nile. It saw the participation of 5,400 British soldiers, who advanced quite slowly on the mighty river. The relief force was attacked several times by the Mahdists, but was able to repel them. Progress was also slowed by the British boats often having to be pulled through rapids by ropes from the shore. The strength of the current made this an extremely complicated and dangerous manoeuvre. Realizing that time was running out for General Gordon and his men, Wolseley split his force into two columns and sent 2,400 men mounted on dromedaries on a 280km shortcut across the desert to Khartoum. Despite Wolseley's efforts, however, the Sudanese capital fell to the besieging Mahdist Army of 50,000 warriors on 26 January 1885. The entire Egyptian garrison was massacred, including General Gordon. Two days later, two British steamers of the relief fleet moving up the Nile reached Khartoum, only to find that the city had fallen. The campaign continued for some other weeks, during which the British land forces moving towards Khartoum were attacked several times by the Mahdists. Being heavily outnumbered, the British troops lacked the supplies to continue campaigning in Sudan and their government decided to order a general retreat towards Egypt. Following his great victories, the Mahdi established an Islamic state governed by Sharia law in Sudan. Although he died just six months later, the Mahdist State survived him. Keen to avenge the death of Gordon, the British government eventually launched a campaign to reconquer

Sudan ten years later in 1895. The lengthy delay in doing so clearly shows how severe the defeat of 1885 at Khartoum had been for both the Egyptians and the British. The Egyptian Army played no significant role in the Nile Expedition, but after 1885 it was tasked with protecting the border of southern Egypt from incursions by the Mahdists. As a result, in the years that followed the fall of Khartoum, it was gradually enlarged.

Egyptian cavalrymen in 1885. They are wearing white summer dress in lancer-style.

In 1890, the Egyptian regular forces was made up of the following units: twelve infantry battalions (eight Egyptian and four Sudanese), one cavalry regiment with six squadrons, one camel corps with three companies, three field artillery batteries, three fortress artillery batteries and one depot battery. In total, the various units contain sixty-five senior British officers. Of the eight Egyptian infantry battalions, one was a depot unit, while the four Sudanese battalions were considered to be the elite of the Egyptian troops due to their great physical qualities and excellent discipline. The twelve infantry battalions were supplemented by a single penal company. The troopers of the cavalry regiment were equipped as lancers. The three field artillery batteries had six guns each; one battery was horse-drawn, one was camel-drawn and one was mule-drawn. During the 1890s, the Egyptian Army continued to expand, mostly in view of the coming confrontation with the Mahdist forces. In 1892 it comprised the following corps: fourteen battalions of infantry (nine made up of Egyptians and five of Sudanese), one cavalry regiment with ten squadrons, one camel corps with three companies, three field artillery batteries, one garrison artillery battalion with three companies and one depot battery. One of the Egyptian infantry battalions was a depot one. In addition to the above, there were some other minor units: three independent cavalry troops acting as the mounted escort of the Khedive, one autonomous elite company of mounted infantry patrolling the southern frontier with Sudan and one penal company of infantry. A conscript could avoid military service in exchange for the payment of a special tax; compulsory service in the regular forces lasted for four years. In 1894, the Egyptian Army was enlarged again and came to comprise the following units: eight battalions of Egyptian infantry, five battalions of Sudanese infantry, on cavalry regiment with eight squadrons, three detachments of the camel corps (two Egyptian and one Sudanese) with two companies each, one horse-drawn field battery, one camel-drawn field battery, one mule-drawn field battery, one fortress artillery battalion with four companies and five train companies with dromedaries. In 1895, in preparation for the campaign to retake Sudan, the Egyptian conscription system was slightly modified, with the traditional exemptions for the inhabitants of Alexandria and Cairo abolished. By the end of 1895, the Egyptian Army had been considerably expanded and could deploy nineteen infantry battalions with six companies each (thirteen Egyptian battalions and six Sudanese battalions), one cavalry regiment with ten squadrons (all made up of Egyptians), one camel corps with four Egyptian and four Sudanese companies, one battery of horse artillery and four batteries of field artillery.

The Sudanese component of the Egyptian Army was becoming increasingly large and important. Indeed, there were several Sudanese officers who could potentially reach the rank of captain. In the years that followed the fall of Khartoum, the Mahdists

Africa 215

Sudanese cavalryman wearing the new khaki campaign dress introduced for the Egyptian Army in 1899. (*ASKB Military Collection*)

were perceived as a serious threat by most of the neighbouring native African countries and European colonial possessions. During 1885 and 1886, the Mahdist State was at war with Abyssinia and – despite suffering several defeats – continued nurturing ambitions to conquer a good portion of Eastern Africa. From 1890, the Mahdists came into conflict with the Italian colony of Eritrea, which had a significant strategic importance due to its location on the Red Sea. The Italians were the first Europeans to defeat the Mahdists on several occasions, notably at the Second Battle of Agordat in December 1893. In 1894, the Italians, together with their native troops recruited in Eritrea, took the important city of Kassala from the Mahdists. A couple of years later, Abyssinia and Italy fought each other for dominance over Eastern Africa, which boosted the Mahdists' expansionist plans. Following these events, and fearing that the French could move from their colonies in sub-Saharan Africa to play a political role in Sudan, the British government finally decided to support Egyptian attempts to reconquer Sudan. General Herbert Kitchener was appointed as overall commander of the Anglo-Egyptian forces that invaded Sudan. Conflict was initiated on 12 March 1896, and a few days later Kitchener's soldiers entered the territory of the Mahdist State. The Anglo-Egyptian expeditionary force consisted of 11,000 soldiers and was supported by a flotilla of gunboats on the Nile. Kitchener's advance was slow and methodical, as the Anglo-Egyptian force built fortified camps along the march as well as narrow-gauge railways. Except for some occasional skirmishing, the early months of the war saw no serious fighting. The first major clash of the conflict was at Farka and ended in a serious defeat for the Mahdists, who lost around 800 warriors. During 1896, the Anglo-Egyptian forces invested the important settlement of Dongola, which was defended by a substantial Mahdist garrison. It was seized in September after Kitchener's men suffered severe losses due to the outbreak of cholera in their camp. With the fall of Dongola, the Mahdist capital of Omdurman started to be menaced by the advancing Anglo-Egyptian army. Consequently, the Mahdists began assembling all their forces (more than 150,000 men) for a decisive battle with the invaders. During their advance, the Anglo-Egyptian troops linked up with the Italian colonial units that were garrisoning Kassala and regained control of the city. Meanwhile, in their south-western possessions, the Mahdists had to face an expedition mounted by the Belgian colony of the Congo Free State. The Belgians considered the Mahdist State a potential threat to the territorial integrity of their Congolese possessions and wanted to gain access to the course of the Nile. They thus decided to collaborate with the British by sending a military expedition against the Mahdists. On 17 February 1897, the Belgians soundly defeated a small Mahdist force at the Battle of Rejaf. In January 1898, after receiving significant reinforcements from Britain and Egypt, Kitchener's troops attacked and defeated a minor Mahdist force at Atbara.

By the late summer of 1898, the Anglo-Egyptian expeditionary force mustered some 26,000 soldiers assembled into two British brigades and four Egyptian brigades. On 2 September 1898, the decisive Battle of Omdurman was fought between the Anglo-Egyptian troops and the Mahdist Army. The Mahdists fielded some 52,000 warriors, but did not have as strong an artillery component as their opponents. The clash began in the early morning with a massive assault by the Mahdists, who suffered severe casualties during their advance, which were mostly caused by the fifty-two quick-firing guns of the Anglo-Egyptian artillery. After more than 4,000 Mahdists had been killed, the Anglo-Egyptian horse-mounted and camel-mounted troops came under attack from an elite force of 15,000 Mahdist warriors. However, the Mahdists were repulsed with heavy losses thanks to accurate fire from two of the gunboats operating on the Nile. After the failure of this second assault, most of the Mahdist Army had been routed, and Kitchener then decided to advance on Omdurman. The British 21st Lancer Regiment was sent ahead to clear the plain in front of the Mahdist capital. After a violent clash, 400 British lancers were able to defeat a force of 2,500 Mahdist warriors in is considered the last great charge in the glorious history of the British cavalry. At this point, the Mahdists mounted a final and desperate counter-attack, which was annihilated by the quick fire of the

Egyptian soldiers of the Camel Corps wearing white campaign dress. On the left, it is possible to see a cavalry officer with summer uniform, while on the right there is a cavalry NCO with winter uniform.

Anglo-Egyptian Maxim machine guns. When the Battle of Omdurman came to an end, more than 11,000 Mahdist soldiers had been killed. The Mahdist capital was soon occupied by Kitchener. The Anglo-Egyptian campaign lasted for several more months, during which the surviving bands of Mahdists still active in southern Sudan were crushed by Anglo-Egyptian forces. By the end of 1899, the last remnants of the Mahdist State had been destroyed and the border between French and British colonial possessions in Sudan was clearly established. The territory of Sudan was not annexed to Egypt but was organized as an Anglo-Egyptian condominium. From a legal point of view, sovereignty and administration were shared between Britain and Egypt, but in practice the Egyptians had only a limited influence over Sudan, which became part of the British colonial system in Africa.

In 1906 the Egyptian Army consisted of the following units: nine Egyptian infantry battalions, six Sudanese infantry battalions, one Railway Battalion (tasked with guarding the railway lines), one Arab Battalion, four Egyptian cavalry squadrons, one Sudanese cavalry squadron, one camel corps (consisting of three companies mounted on dromedaries and one company on mules), one machine gun company, four field artillery batteries transported on mules and three companies of garrison artillery. The Arab Battalion, stationed in Kassala, was an irregular camel corps that was made up of locally raised auxiliaries (from the Hadendoa and Bani Amer communities). It had two companies and, being considered a frontier force tasked with patrolling the south-eastern border of Sudan, included a number of British officers and NCOs. Service in the active army lasted for five years, which were followed by a period of five years in the reserve. Recruitment of conscripts was by ballot, with a man liable for compulsory service between the ages of 22 and 26. There were, however, several ways to be exempted from military service: it was possible, for example, to pay a special tax before balloting. A series of social groups and categories were also exempt from compulsory service: employees of the state, sons of military officers, individuals having serious family problems and members of some religious minorities. The Sudanese battalions were the best quality of the Egyptian infantry, helped by all their superior officers being British. In total, the Egyptian Army had around 18,000 soldiers, including 140 British officers and NCOs. In 1911, a conscript's period of service in the active army was reduced to three years. It should be noted that during the whole post-1882 period, Sudanese soldiers serving in the Egyptian Army were not recruited by conscription but enlisted as volunteers. By 1912, the Egyptian military comprised the following corps: nine Egyptian infantry battalions with four companies each, seven Sudanese infantry battalions with six companies each, two independent companies of mounted infantry, one Bedouin Battalion (the previous Arab Battalion), two Egyptian cavalry squadrons, one Sudanese cavalry squadron,

Sudanese private (left) and NCO (right) of the Camel Corps; they are dressed with the standard dark blue uniform worn by the infantry of the Egyptian Army during cold months.

one camel corps with four Egyptian companies and one Sudanese company, one machine gun company, four field artillery batteries transported on mules, three garrison artillery companies and one battalion of engineers. In 1913, the Egyptian conscription system was modified, the period of compulsory service in the regular army being increased to six years, followed by another five in the reserve. The usual exemptions continued. Each infantry battalion was commanded by an officer known as a *kaimakam* and was sub-divided into two wings; in the Egyptian battalions, each of the latter had two companies, while in the Sudanese battalions they had three companies. A company, commanded by an officer known as a *youzbashee*, was sub-divided into two half-companies, each of which consisted of two platoons. One sapper was included in each infantry company. One of the Sudanese infantry battalions was known as the Equatorial Battalion, tasked with garrisoning the south-western portion of Sudan in Equatorial Africa. The cavalry squadrons each had four platoons, and a single platoon was sub-divided into three eight-man squads. All the Egyptian and Sudanese cavalrymen were equipped as lancers. The new Engineer Battalion was the previous Railway Battalion, consisting of twelve companies in time of peace, but could be rapidly enlarged to sixteen companies. The unit acted as the labour force of the Egyptian Army. In addition to the units described above, there was the small Guard of the Khedive, with two infantry companies and one cavalry squadron. In 1914, the various units of the Egyptian Army were distributed as follows around Egypt and Sudan:

- Cairo District: three infantry battalions, one cavalry squadron, one field artillery battery and one company of garrison artillery
- Atbara District: one infantry battalion
- Khartoum District: seven infantry battalions, three independent companies of mounted infantry, one cavalry squadron, four field artillery batteries and two companies of garrison artillery
- Wad Madani District: one infantry battalion and one company of the camel corps
- El Obeid District: one infantry battalion, one company of the camel corps and one field artillery battery
- Talodi: one infantry battalion
- Tanfikia: one infantry battalion
- Mongalla: five infantry companies from the Equatorial Battalion
- Wan: one infantry battalion
- Kassala: one infantry half-battalion, the Arab Battalion and one artillery detachment
- Port Sudan: one infantry half-battalion and one artillery detachment

Most of the units thus garrisoned the vast territory of Sudan, with the overall composition of the Egyptian Army having been slightly changed from that of 1912. The Egyptian contribution to the British war effort during the First World War was negligible, despite the fact that Britain and the Ottoman Empire fought in the Sinai

Contemporary print showing the uniforms of the Egyptian infantry and artillery in the late nineteenth century. On the left is a Krupp field gun, while on the right is a British officer with khaki campaign dress. As this picture shows, the white summer dress, dark blue winter dress and khaki campaign dress were often used at the same time.

Peninsula for possession of the Suez Canal. The defence of the canal from the Turkish offensives was entirely assigned to the British Army. The Egyptians provided just a few field artillery batteries during 1915. A single field artillery battery of the Egyptian Army, supported by a small detachment of machine guns, was later sent to the Arabian Peninsula to support the local insurgents in their uprising against the Ottomans. It should be noted, however, that thousands of Egyptian civilians contributed with their hard work to Britain's war effort. During the Great War, the British created two paramilitary auxiliary corps that mostly consisted of impressed Egyptian civilians: the Egyptian Labour Corps (with 88,000 men) and Camel Transport Corps (96,000 men). The presence of the Egyptian Army in Sudan also enabled the British to employ all their troops in North Africa at the front, with normal garrison duties being performed by the Egyptians. The Sudanese military units remained part of the Egyptian Army until 1925, when the autonomous Sudan Defence Force was created after a major mutiny of the Sudanese troops in Egyptian service.

Chapter 9

The Mediterranean

Malta

Great Britain had controlled the strategic Mediterranean archipelago of Malta since 1800, when British troops liberated it from the French occupation that had begun two years earlier. Prior to 1798, Malta had been an independent nation ruled by the Order of St John, which had transformed it into a bastion of Christianity in the Mediterranean as well as a significant naval power. Until 1813, Malta was a British protectorate. It was then transformed into a Crown Colony and was governed as such despite being located in Europe. The British knew that controlling Malta gave them an important base for the Royal Navy in the central Mediterranean, so the island always had a significant military garrison. During the Napoleonic Wars, several locally raised corps were formed in Malta, but these were all disbanded by 1815 with the final defeat of Napoleon. As a result, it was decided in that year to form a new unit known as the Royal Malta Fencible Regiment. This acted both as the military garrison of Malta as well as a police force tasked with keeping order on the island. The regiment could not be deployed outside its home territory and comprised many veterans of the Napoleonic Wars. It consisted of ten companies, seven of which acted as line infantry, while the remaining three were coastal artillery units. By 1854, the number of companies had been reduced to six (three of infantry and three of artillery), but the Royal Malta Fencible Regiment continued to be scattered in various independent detachments across its homeland. In 1854, a veteran company was formed, the Royal Malta Fencible Pensioners Company, which was made up of former members of the Royal Malta Fencible Regiment who were still capable of performing static garrison duties. It continued to exist until 1861, when the Royal Malta Fencible Regiment was converted into a garrison artillery corps and receiving the new name of the Royal Malta Fencible Artillery. In addition to the units described above, for a few years Malta was also garrisoned by its militia, which was reorganized by the British in 1852. This consisted of just six infantry companies, which were disbanded during 1857 due to the local population's lack of enthusiasm for military service. In 1853, the British organized a locally raised auxiliary corps known as the Malta Dockyard Battalion of Artillery, which was tasked with defending the

The Mediterranean

NCO of the Royal Malta Fencible Regiment in the early 1850s.

Private of the Royal Malta Fencible Pensioners Company in 1854. The uniform is the standard one worn by all the Corps of Invalids of the British Army.

Officer with pillbox cap and patrol jacket (left) and officer in parade dress (right) of the Royal Malta Fencible Artillery in 1876. (*ASKB Military Collection*)

important dockyards of Malta and consisted of individuals who had been exempted from militia service. The new battalion comprised three sub-units: the Dockyard Company, the Victualling Company and the Factory Company. Members of the corps were trained to act as coastal artillerymen, but mostly performed as dock workers. The Malta Dockyard Battalion of Artillery was disbanded in 1864. The Royal Malta Fencible Artillery remained the only locally raised military corps in

Malta for a long time. It provided 100 volunteers to the British Army in 1882 for the war against Egypt, and in 1889 it was renamed as the Royal Malta Artillery. In 1889, the Maltese militia was re-formed as the Royal Malta Regiment of Militia, which assumed the new denomination of the King's Own Malta Regiment in 1903. The unit, consisting of ten companies tasked with performing garrison duties, continued to exist until 1921. The Royal Malta Artillery was disbanded only in 1970, a few years before Malta became completely independent from Britain.

Gibraltar, Ionian Islands and Cyprus

The Rock of Gibraltar, located on the southern tip of the Iberian Peninsula and dominating the strait that connects the Mediterranean Sea with the Atlantic Ocean, was captured by Britain from Spain in 1704. Since then, due to the frequent Spanish attacks that took place during the eighteenth century, Britain's western Mediterranean stronghold – extremely small but very important strategically – was always garrisoned by regular units of the British Army. The first locally raised military corps of Gibraltar – the Gibraltar Volunteer Corps – was formed only in 1915 during the First World War. To this day, Gibraltar is still an Overseas Territory of Great Britain. In 1797, France defeated the Republic of Venice in Italy and occupied the Ionian Islands of Greece, which had long been part of the Mediterranean possessions of the Venetians. The Ionian Islands – Corfu, Paxoi, Zakynthos, Cephalonia, Lefkada, Ithaca and Kythira – are located between southern Italy and the coastline of western Greece, making them of great naval importance as they control entry to the Adriatic Sea. The French occupied the Ionian Islands from 1797–1799, when a joint Russian and Ottoman expeditionary force captured them. In 1800, the Ionian archipelago was reorganized as the Septinsular Republic, a semi-autonomous oligarchic republic that was dominated by Russia. In 1807, the new state lost its independence and ceased to exist,

Foot gendarme of the Cyprus Military Police in 1878. The uniform is in perfect Ottoman style.

Mounted gendarme (NCO) of the Cyprus Military Police in 1903. The equipment of the horse is in Ottoman fashion.

Russia ceding the Ionian Islands to Napoleonic France in accordance with the Treaty of Tilsit. Between 1809 and 1814, the Royal Navy progressively took all the islands of the archipelago from the French. In 1815, the Ionian Islands were reorganized as the United States of the Ionian Islands, a semi-autonomous British protectorate. This continued to exist until 1864, when the Ionian Islands were finally ceded by Britain to the Kingdom of Greece. Between 1815 and 1864, no locally raised military units were formed by the British in the United States of the Ionian Islands, despite the fact that the latter's constitution – promulgates declared in 1817 – prescribed the creation of a local militia tasked with performing police duties. The large Mediterranean island of Cyprus, located south of Turkey, became a British protectorate in 1878 following the Russo-Turkish War of 1877–1878. The Ottoman Empire, having been soundly defeated by the Russians, preserved part of its territorial integrity only thanks to the diplomatic support of Great Britain, but in exchange for this it had to cede Cyprus to the British. The island was always garrisoned by British regular troops and soon became an important station for the Royal Navy, being formally transformed into a Crown Colony in 1915. In 1878, the British raised a paramilitary police force in Cyprus known as the Cyprus Military Police, which mostly consisted of former Ottoman policemen and was tasked with keeping order on the island. In 1879, the British formed an auxiliary military unit, the Cyprus Pioneers, to undertake works of public utility, but this was soon absorbed into the Cyprus Military Police. The latter came to comprise 220 mounted policemen and 470 foot policemen, who had British officers. By 1890, half of the policemen came from the Greek communities of Cyprus and half from the communities of the Turkish minority.

Bibliography

Abbott, P., *Colonial Armies in Africa 1850–1918* (Foundry Books, 2009)
Barthorp, M., *Indian Infantry Regiment 1860–1914* (Osprey Publishing, 1979)
Barthorp, M., *The British Troops in the Indian Mutiny 1857–1859* (Osprey Publishing, 1994)
Bayley, C.C., *Mercenaries for the Crimea: The German, Swiss and Italian Legions in British Service 1854–1856* (Queen's University Press, 1977)
Boulton, J.J., *Uniforms of the Canadian Mounted Police* (Turner Warwick Publications, 1990)
Carman, W.Y., *Indian Army Uniforms Under the British: Artillery, Engineers and Infantry* (Morgan-Grampian, 1969)
Carman, W.Y., *Indian Army Uniforms Under the British: Cavalry* (Leonardhill Books, 1961)
Castle, I., *Zulu War Volunteers, Irregulars and Auxiliaries* (Osprey Publishing, 2003)
Chappell, M., *The Gurkhas* (Osprey Publishing, 1994)
Chartrand, R., *British Forces in North America 1793–1815* (Osprey Publishing, 1998)
Chartrand, R., *British Forces in the West Indies 1793–1815* (Osprey Publishing, 1996)
Chartrand, R., *Victoria's Canadian Militia* (Service Publications, 2016)
Chesney, A.G., *Historical Records of the Maltese Corps of the British Army* (Clowes and Sons, 1897)
Festberg, A.N. and Videon, B.J., *Uniforms of the Australian Colonies* (Hill of Content, 1972)
French, J., *The British in India 1825 to 1859* (Foundry Books, 2006)
Goodspeed, D.J., *The Armed Forces of Canada 1867–1967* (Directorate of History of the Canadian Forces, 1967)
Harris, R.G., *Bengal Cavalry Regiments 1857–1914* (Osprey Publishing, 1979)
Head, R. and McClenaghan, T., *The Maharajas' Paltans: A History of the Indian State Forces (1888–1948)* (Manohar Publishers, 2013)
Heath, I., *Armies of the 19th Century: China* (Foundry Books, 2009)
Heath, I., *The North-East Frontier 1837–1901* (Osprey Publishing, 1999)
Heath, I., *The Taiping Rebellion 1851–1866* (Osprey Publishing, 1994)
Knight, I., *Australian Bushrangers 1788–1880* (Osprey Publishing, 2019)
Knight, I., *Boer Wars 1836–1898* (Osprey Publishing, 1996)
Knight, I., *Boer Wars 1898–1902* (Osprey Publishing, 1996)
Knight, I., *British Forces in Zululand 1879* (Osprey Publishing, 1991)
Knight, I., *The New Zealand Wars 1820–1872* (Osprey Publishing, 2013)
Lord, C. and Birtles, D., *The Armed Forces of Aden and the Protectorate 1839–1967* (Helion & Company, 2011)
McBride, A., *The Zulu War* (Osprey Publishing, 1976)
Mollo, B., *The Indian Army* (Blandford Press, 1981)
Montague, R., *Dress and Insignia of the British Army in Australia and New Zealand, 1770–1870* (Library of Australian History, 1981)

Nicholson, J.B.R., *The Gurkha Rifles* (Osprey Publishing, 1974)
Reid, S., *Armies of the East India Company 1750–1850* (Osprey Publishing, 2009)
Ross, D. and Tyler, G., *Canadian Campaigns 1860–1870* (Osprey Publishing, 1992)
Rothero, C., *Skinner's Horse* (Almark, 1979)
Roubicek, M., *Early Modern Arab Armies* (Franciscan Press, 1977)
Tylden, G., *The Armed Forces of South Africa 1659–1954* (Trophy Press, 1982)
Wedd, M., *Australian Military Uniforms 1800–1982* (Kangaroo Press, 1982)
Wilkinson-Latham, C., *North-West Frontier 1837–1947* (Osprey Publishing, 1977)
Wilkinson-Latham, C., *The Indian Mutiny* (Osprey Publishing, 1977)
Winsley, T.M., *A History of the Singapore Volunteer Corps, 1854–1937* (Singapore, 1938)

Index

Auckland, 82

Berbice, 50, 59
Bikaner, 174

Coote Manningham, 11

Demerara, 51, 59
Diggers, 67–9

Essequibo, 50, 59

Flagstaff War, 80
Frederick Haldimand, 10

Great Trek, 87, 93

Henri Bouquet, 10
Hunters' Lodge, 23

Jacques Prevost, 10
James Skinner, 121

Klondike, 43
kukri, 127, 144

Mad Mullah, 206
Monongahela, Battle of, 8, 10

Navy Island, 23
Nyasaland, 202–203, 206

Patriot Party, 22
Plassey, 105, 112, 115
Prince Albert, 13, 91

Rangoon, 182
Rum Corps, The, 61

Sarawak, 185, 187, 189
Septinsular Republic, 225
Sillidar System, 125, 138

Vinegar Hill, 62

Winnipeg, 33

Yukon, 43

Dear Reader,

We hope you have enjoyed this book, but why not share your views on social media? You can also follow our pages to see more about our other products: facebook.com/penandswordbooks or follow us on X @penswordbooks

You can also view our products at www.pen-and-sword.co.uk (UK and ROW) or www.penandswordbooks.com (North America).

To keep up to date with our latest releases and online catalogues, please sign up to our newsletter at: www.pen-and-sword.co.uk/newsletter

If you would like a printed catalogue with our latest books, then please email: enquiries@pen-and-sword.co.uk or telephone: 01226 734555 (UK and ROW) or email: uspen-and-sword@casematepublishers.com or telephone: (610) 853-9131 (North America).

We respect your privacy and we will only use personal information to send you information about our products.

Thank you!